- Catholic church - doctrines. adresses, essays, lectures
- Sex- religious aspects - Catholic church Adresses, essays, lectures
- Sexual ethics - Addresses, essays, lectures

HUMAN SEXUALITY IN OUR TIME
What the Church Teaches

HUMAN SEXUALITY
in Our Time

WHAT THE CHURCH TEACHES

Edited by
George A. Kelly

ST. PAUL EDITIONS

NIHIL OBSTAT
Rev. Richard V. Lawlor, S.J.

IMPRIMATUR
+ Humberto Cardinal Medeiros
Archbishop of Boston

The Nihil Obstat and Imprimatur are official declarations that a
book or pamphlet is free of doctrinal or moral error. No implication is
contained therein that those who have granted the Nihil Obstat and
Imprimatur agree with the contents, opinions or statements expressed.

Library of Congress Cataloging in Publication Data

Human sexuality in our time—What the Church teaches

Lectures given by the faculty of the Institute for Advanced
Studies in Catholic Doctrine at St. John's University during the
spring of 1978.

Includes index.

1. Sex and religion—Addresses, essays, lectures. 2. Sexual
ethics—Addresses, essays, lectures. 3. Catholic Church—Doctrinal
works—Addresses, essays, lectures. I. Kelly, George Anthony, 1916—
II. St. John's University, New York. Institute for Advanced
Studies in Catholic Doctrine.

HQ63.H8   261.8'34'1   79-15114

Printed in the U.S.A. by the Daughters of St. Paul
50 St. Paul's Ave., Jamaica Plain, Boston, Ma. 02130

The Daughters of St. Paul are an international congregation of religious
women serving the Church with the communications media.

CONTENTS

These lectures were given by the faculty of the **Institute for Advanced Studies in Catholic Doctrine** at St. John's University during the Spring of 1978. They were intended as an enrichment course for graduate students pursuing a Master's Degree in Catholic Doctrine, which the University grants under its charter from the state of New York. Successful candidates also receive a teaching certificate from the Holy See, which prompted St. John's University to establish the Institute in 1974.

The Editor

CHAPTER ONE

The Bitter Pill
the Catholic Community Swallowed*

Rev. Msgr. George A. Kelly

1. The Background

The pill was contraception.

How the Catholic Church lost the support of its people over this matter is a story still to be told with finality. But lost many of its people to contraception the Church did and in a very few years.

Father Andrew Greeley lately (1976) has announced with ferocious certainty that the deterioration in American Catholicism is due to the encyclical *(Humanae vitae)* which in 1968 upheld the Church's ban on contraception. Greeley has a chapter in his *Catholic Schools in a Declining Church* which "proves" by mathematical formula that what he has been saying since 1968 is true: A continued ban on contraception was a disaster for the American Church (p. 316).

That book itself deserves comment later, but for the purposes of this chapter it is sufficient to say that the Greeley thesis can be maintained as a working hypothesis only if "the contraceptive issue" is seen—not as a single item—but as a "mixed bag" of many Catholic issues which were the subject of fierce attack before, during, and after Vatican II. Although the direct confrontations

---

*Excerpted from *The Battle for the American Church* by Msgr. George A. Kelly. Reprinted by permission of Doubleday and Company, Inc.

seemed at first to center on steroid pills such as Enovid and Ortho-Novum, later on condoms and diaphrams, the basic controversy was always over more basic questions: What is the law of God? What is the will of Christ? Who says so and with what authority?

Those priests and married couples who after World War II organized what was the most successful family life apostolate in the history of the American Church saw their work crumble within the space of a few years. The Cana and Pre-Cana Conferences, the Christian Family Movement, the Cana Clubs and Holy Family Guilds, the Marriage Preparation Courses, Family Consultation Centers, Marriage Counselling, training of priests, regular attention to Catholic family life by all Catholic magazines, especially *Sign* and *America*, under the respective editorships of Father Ralph Gorman, C.P., and Father Thurston Davis, S.J., were the crests of rock-like Catholic family formations which supported the Catholic family value system, by then a lonely isle in an all-embracing surrounding sea of broken homes, one-two child families, rising rates of illegitimacy, divorce, abortion. Sociologist John L. Thomas, S.J., wrote a pioneer book *The Catholic Family* which laid out the ingredients necessary to protect the identity and future of the Catholic Family system as a viable sub-culture when the power of secularized culture was overwhelming. Continuing education, mechanisms of motivation and regular support systems were the instruments by which the Church kept Catholic family life intact and guaranteed its future.

Looking backward from the time when the American bishops created the *Family Life Bureau* in the *National Catholic Welfare Conference* (1931) to the eve of the Second Vatican Council (1961), the rise and rapid growth of the Family Life apostolate was phenomenal. In fact, this apostolate seemed to take off all by itself (sometimes without bishops knowing what was going on), as if parish priests (most of the early organizers were priests) and married couples were driven by a compulsive need to survive as a Catholic body. In view of the bitterness later demonstrated by Catholic contraceptionists, a flashback to those days only reveals enthusiasm, love of the Church, outpourings of energy on behalf of *The Word*.

And *The Word* was what the Church said it was (including the rejection of contraception). Not only were the private discussions and the nationwide network of Cana, Pre-Cana, and CFM meetings positive in their exploration and appreciation of Catholic family values, but the literature was also formative and enthusiastic. John Delaney, editor for Doubleday, published a book in 1958 designed to show that Catholic family values were not "the imposition of the will of a few cranky clerics on the Catholic populace" and to show further that "there is nothing arbitrary about the Church's stand" on marriage matters. The book was John L. Thomas' *The Catholic Viewpoint on Marriage and the Family*. Rereading Father Thomas' exposition of the "Catholic Problem" offers *prima facie* evidence of how secure Catholic scholars were then interpreting not only the mind of the Church but the mood and needs of Catholic people. What was the source of the Catholic problem in 1958? Father Thomas listed a few: (1) the sixteenth-century denial of the sacramental bond of marriage; (2) the gradual rejection of the influence of religious doctrine on the formation of marriage and family values; (3) the tendency of social scientists to look upon the human person as nothing more than a complex combination of basic urges, conditioned reflexes, and acquired habits; (4) the American habit of being "practical" in judgment without necessary reference to principle or doctrine (pp. 25-27).

In the face of the practical options being offered at that time to marrieds and about-to-be marrieds in America, on what did the special Catholic family system depend? According to Thomas: on its clearly defined but distinctive set of ideals, standards, and patterns of conduct related to sex and marriage. Said Thomas in 1958: "If you want to know why people judge certain family practices to be right or wrong you must find out how they define the nature and purpose of marriage. If you want to understand why they define marriage as they do, you must discover their view of human nature. In the final analysis, therefore, all definitions of human values are ultimately derived from some view of man, the human agent. If people hold different views concerning the origin, nature and destiny of man, they will logically define the purposes of marriage differently and will develop different patterns of conduct in relationship to marriage" (p. 23). For almost two hundred pages Father Thomas proceeds to explain why Catholics do not agree with other Americans on the essential purposes of marriage, the moral laws regulating marital relations and the use of sex outside of marriage.

In those halcyon days it was clear that the marital issue separating Catholics from non-Catholics was not the condom or the diaphram but a cluster of issues having to do with the sacred elements of human nature and the Church's understanding of God's revelation. Popes Pius XI and XII frequently used terms like "divine institution," "divine design," "divinely established order," when speaking of many subject areas of religious thought. Contraception was only one of them. As seculars first, then more and more Protestants and Jews, moved away from these notions, behavioral patterns changed with the changed concepts. The Catholic world view, on the other hand, retained the "wholeness" which underpinned its family life. However, when tampering began either with a practice (contraception) or with an idea (divine design), it was inevitable that changed behavior would call for changed ideas, and vice versa also. Even if the average Catholic did not always understand the connection between mind and conduct, Father Thomas saw this quite clearly.

However, assertions about the coherence of the Catholic family value system or the Church's struggle to make it operative in the lives of people led to the following practical questions: Did the Church's labors succeed? Did Catholics actually live by the Church's book?

Almost all priests who heard confessions or were effective parochial pastors of souls in the past half century would agree that the answers to both questions were yes. Family Life directors of any major diocese, also, where sexual aberrations among the faithful were always higher, can bear witness that the best Catholic family apostolates in the nation were precisely in the large metropolitan centers where the pressures on couples, old and young, were most severe.

But there is still a better witness to what was going on in American Catholic family life prior to 1962.

He is Andrew Greeley.

In the Spring of 1963, Father Greeley wrote an article for *Chicago Studies* entitled "Family Planning Among American Catholics." He was not yet ten years a priest and still a curate at Christ the King parish in Chicago.

The Chicago Studies article bases its conclusions on two secular studies—one a 1959 Michigan Study—the other a 1961 Princeton Study, through which Greeley hoped to demolish "some favorite myths about Catholic family planning." He reported as follows:

1. Concerning the myth that most Catholic families really do not accept the Church's teaching on birth control, Greeley says: "The Michigan Study shows the contrary to be true: *Catholics accept the Church's teaching with a vengeance*" (italics mine).

Only 32% of Catholics gave unqualified approval to birth control, compared to 72% of Protestants and 88% of Jews.

Greeley concludes that on the subject of family limitation "Some Catholic respondents were more Catholic than the Church."

2. Concerning the myth that family-limiting Catholics use methods condemned by the Church, Greeley reports that only 30% used contraceptives.

Only 22% of regular Mass-goers used contraception.

3. Greeley concludes: "Religious affiliation is a very powerful determinant of behavior in this

area—the success of Church efforts to induce the
younger generation of Catholic couples to adopt approved methods [contradicts] assertions occasionally
made that Catholics are increasingly adopting ap-
pliance methods."

4. Concerning the myth that upper-class
Catholics more likely adopt contraception, Greeley
concludes: "The more education, the more income,
the higher the occupational category, the more likely Catholics are to keep the Church's law and the
more likely they are to have or to want larger
families."

5. Concerning the myth that periodic continence is an inefficient method of family limitation,
Greeley estimates: "The rhythm method is not
drastically less efficient than the others."

Greeley also warns the reader that "such studies do
not merit the same kind of acceptance as would, let us
say, mathematical demonstrations or experiments in the
physical or biological sciences." In defending the professional integrity of sociologists, he chides those who think
"that demographers do not understand the consistency of
the Church's teaching on sex and procreation, that they
do not have a respect for the Catholic conscience, that
they expect the Church to change its position, or that
they expect Catholics to violate their moral principles."
Greeley's article may have demolished myths but it also
underlined the existence of Catholic moral principles on
contraception, a Catholic conscience on the subject, and
a Church firmly committed to its principles.

From this high plateau of adherence and practical
observance there followed a precipitous decline among
Catholics within the ten-year period following 1963. Obviously, something more was at work than a new
Catholic desire to use a condom, a diaphragm or a pill.
The Catholic people earlier under equally adverse social
pressures—the Great Depression and the Great
Wars—continued to recognize contraception as a sinful
use of marriage. Something else must have happened
after 1961.

2. The Catholic People Are Indoctrinated

Many things were going on in the Catholic community relative to contraception since the post-war baby boom began to alarm population experts. In 1944, government statistician Oliver E. Baker was declaring demography to be the most exact of the social sciences. He also predicted (on the basis of statistical computations) the leveling off of population growth in the United States. But people changed the numbers by placing high value on parenthood. Whereas in 1936, 1,000 women aged 15-44 bore 76 children, a similar cohort of women bore 121 children in 1956. Later demographers coined words such as "population explosion," "the population bomb," "standing room only" to make their point that planned parenthood (soon to be euphemistically retitled "responsible parenthood") was now as much a requirement for Americans, as it was for third world peasants.

The tools of persuasion would be more sophisticated but the motivation was similar to that made into a crusade years earlier by Margaret Sanger. During the depth of the depression, when almost one quarter of all women of childbearing age had no children at all, the founder of the birth control movement wrote an article for *The American Weekly* (May 27, 1934) in which she proposed an "American Baby Code." The essential ingredients of her philosophy are found in the following articles:

> "Article 3. A marriage shall in itself give husband and wife only the rights to a common household and not the right to parenthood.
> "Article 4. No woman shall have the legal right to bear a child and no man shall have the right to become a father without a permit for parenthood....
> "Article 6. No permit shall be valid for more than one birth."

These embarrassing statements are now buried in library stacks, but Mrs. Sanger's haunting fears of unwanted and unneeded babies have worked their way into the psyche of American intellectuals and through them into the souls of mothers and prospective mothers. Yet technical advances, which provided unmarried and married adults alike the power to separate sexual activity from parenthood, did not automatically mean social approval of contraception or widespread dissemination of devices, as long as there was popular consensus that contraception was evil. In fact, the "Protestant ethic" about contraception was frequently enforced by written and unwritten laws. Contraceptives could not be sent through the mails, they could not be advertised (although obtainable at the back of drugstores), they could not be sold to minors or the unmarried, nor could birth control advice be given in public hospitals. Those restrictions lasted as long as the religious consensus lasted—that is, up until the late 1950's.

The birth control crusaders, however, were not without determination. They had begun as early as 1908 working to persuade the Church of England to give at least limited endorsement of the use of contraceptives by Christians. Successively they were turned down by the Lambeth Conferences of 1908 and 1920, but gained sympathetic hearing from some Anglican bishops for exceptional use of contraception in abnormal cases." This was the view which prevailed at Lambeth in 1930 when for the first time a prominent Christian body, while still insisting that "the primary and obvious method is complete abstinence (as far as may be necessary) in a life of discipline and self-control lived in the power of the Holy Spirit," gave permission for contraceptive use in abnormal cases. Contraception, hereafter, for Anglicans was a tolerated practice, though still without approval. Once this breakthrough was accomplished, further dispensations from standard Anglican behavior were readily granted. The Lambeth Conference of 1958 favored "a positive acceptance of the use of contraceptives within Christian marriage and family life." This is the first time contraception is seen as enriching married life, that the

term "responsible parenthood" is introduced to the ecclesial vocabulary, that family planning is raised to the
status of noble duty. The revolution within Protestantism
was complete. (Five years later a booklet entitled *Toward
a Quaker View of Sex* would reject almost the traditional
approach of the organized Christian sexual morality,
specifically its *a priori* judgments about fornication,
adultery, and homosexuality.)

It is not without significance that in the late fifties an
organized effort was made—successfully as it turned
out—to put the medical profession in the forefront of a
birth control campaign to break down all written or unwritten resistance to contraceptive advice or clinical
assistance for clients. The effort was first made in New
York in 1956, then in Denver, Maryland, Chicago. By
1959 the *American Public Health Association* was on
record in favor of birth control services. The White House
Conference on Children and Youth followed this lead in
1960. By 1961, John D. Rockefeller III was in favor of
government supported birth control programs. Simultaneous, but less spectacular, was the success in making
the social workers employed by the network of bureaus of
public assistance agents of contraceptive advice. The
public relations stress was on freedom for the client, but
the welfare recipient was not unmindful of the social
world's position.

These political efforts were accompanied by widespread public relations programs and intensive lobbying.
Planned Parenthood still encountered some resistance in
high places. One of its setbacks came when William H.
Draper, an investment banker and Planned Parenthood
activist, heading up a government committee, released a
report (July 24, 1959) calling for government financed
and managed population programs. Draper avoided the
words "birth control" and stressed the word "request,"
but it was clear that the *International Planned Parenthood Federation* wanted the United States government to
endorse and underwrite its worldwide efforts to "sell"
contraception. While Catholic politicians such as John

Kennedy and Edmund Brown walked a tightrope on the subject, President Dwight D. Eisenhower buried the Draper Report, banned all government family planning assistance for the duration of his term, with the comment that nothing was more improper for government than activity of this type.

But if Eisenhower was firmer on the subject of cr traception than other politicians, Planned Parenthood came to recognize the vulnerability of public office-holders on this issue, particularly Catholics. Though the U.S. Catholic bishops immediately (1959) warned the public that Catholics would not support assistance programs which promote artificial birth prevention, Planned Parenthood stepped up their campaign to change public opinion. They held a *World Population Emergency Conference* in 1960, took out full-page ads soliciting $1,120,000 to promote the plans of the Draper Committee, brought Margaret Sanger out of retirement (June 14, 1960) as a fund-raiser, and induced the *National Council of Churches in the USA* to take positions favorable not only to contraception but to sterilization as well *(New York Times,* February 24, 1961, p. 16). The NCC statement justified its endorsements on the basis of "the general Protestant conviction that the motives rather than the methods form the primary moral issue." (The editorial comment of *America* [March 11, 1961] on the NCC statement reads: "At stake in these matters is not merely the integrity of marriage; but the very nature of morality. Christian morality is increasingly penetrated by the tendency to scuttle all objective norms of conduct and rationalize the flight from the absolute by appeals to the spirit of the gospel.")

Planned Parenthood also realized the importance of enlisting for their campaign important public figures. By 1962 they had former Secretary of State Christian Herter taking up their cause. As an Episcopalian gentleman of some standing, he came to Planned Parenthood's annual conference in New York to be a bridge to the Catholic community. Herter told his audience that it was no longer correct to think that discussion of the population crisis was offensive to Catholics. He counted on the new ecumenical atmosphere, which Pope John XXIII encouraged, to help because the Vatican is well aware that the issue of birth control is one of the most important bars to a reunion of Catholics and Protestants (*New York Herald Tribune*, October 28, 1962).

The Planned Parenthood leadership had made a significant gesture toward its only formidable opponent—the Catholic Church. The key through the door of the Church was to be "dialogue." At first, Planned Parenthood's leaders did not expect to have any radical effect on the Catholic doctrinal positions, hoping merely to debilitate whatever political force was left in the anti-contraception movement. They took advantage of the fact that Catholic jurisprudence allowed greater leeway in public law for moral evil than Comstock legislators did. The distinction between the propriety of public policy in a plural society from the moral positions of its citizens was well-known. Catholic experts like John Courtney Murray and Gustave Weigel, professors from Woodstock, bishops like Cardinal Suenens were quoted liberally as if they blessed the political aspirations of Planned Parenthood. Another Catholic distinction also came into play, viz. between responsible parenthood and contraception. Catholics were comfortable with the differences. Stress came to be laid on research to develop morally acceptable methods of family limitation. This was a soothing proposal in 1962, even though comparatively little money or results have since been realized.

In the dialogues between Planned Parenthood and Catholic family life leaders after 1958 the following subjects were *never* discussed: the virtues of the unplanned family, the positive values of motherhood, the rejection of contraceptive use by teenagers. (Ten years later Planned Parenthood Federation launched a $4,000,000 two-year program to have available in New York City contraceptive counselling and service to every teenager.) In the early stages of dialogue subjects like sterilization and abortion were soft pedaled. Planned Parenthood officials did not say publicly what some would admit privately, viz. that there was then (even more now) greater reliability for family limitation through natural family planning than for at least half the contraceptives on the market. Probably, the most troubling part of the one-sided dialogue in 1962 was Planned Parenthood's downgrading of the risks of "the pill." Most doctors, when asked, rejected the notion of giving "the pill" to their wives or daughters. The British Medical Society was already facing up to its harmful effects on women who took them. But Dr. Alan F. Guttmacher was dismissing this evidence arguing that potential risks (like heart attacks, embolisms, cancer) had to be balanced against the risks of child-bearing. Twenty years later, as "the pill" diminished in popularity (for its proven dangers to women's health and longevity), Planned Parenthood came under criticism for this neglect.

Yet at one point of dialogue "the pill" was the putative "savior" of interfaith cooperation on birth control. The "pill" might provide the natural planning acceptable to Catholics. Not a few Catholics swallowed this pill.

Planned Parenthood had quietly been working on selected Catholics for some time prior to 1962. "Leading Catholic members" of the *American Public Health Association* were credited with helping draft a pro-birth control resolution as early as 1959. During 1960 the Federation polled 166 Catholic educators, lawyers, editors and public officials seeking a sense of Catholic lay opinion. They found more than half of their interviewers (while asserting Catholic orthodoxy on the subject) ready to accept a tolerant public policy, if that is what non-Catholics wanted. The news media, naturally, made much of this release, as they did earlier of the Draper Report. Panel discussions and interviews with disgruntled welfare clients who (allegedly) could not obtain birth control information became quite common with the Catholic Church always pictured as the ogre interfering with freedom.

By 1962 Planned Parenthood extended their forays deeply into Catholic territory. The Reverend William Genne of the *National Council of Churches* and Mr. Naomi Gray of the *Planned Parenthood* staff appeared at the *National Catholic Family Life Convention* in St. Louis. Other representatives sought meetings with leading Catholic family life directors throughout the country or made trips to Europe seeking dialogue and understanding from leading Catholics in the ancient citadels of Christendom. One internal memorandum (of Planned Parenthood), not intended for public consumption, recapped each visit with a paragraph on how "Father X" or "Monsignor Y" looked at the problem. It was obvious that Planned Parenthood expected support for its objectives from people inside the Catholic University of Louvain (Belgium) and within the Vatican itself. In the cited memorandum one described visit to (a poorly concealed) Msgr. Luigi Ligutti in Rome (Ligutti then being a leading American rural life expert) is interpreted as indicating how sympathetic prelates could be in the Holy City itself. Cass Canfield, chairman of the Editorial Board of Harper and Brothers, and the most sophisticated promoter of Planned Parenthood's cause, was so encouraged by his conversations with officials at the Vatican that in a letter dated July 5, 1962, he extended an invitation to Msgr. John C. Knott, the American bishops' national director of family life, to become one of four Catholics who would dialogue with eight non-Catholics, in part to show that the area of differences between Catholics and non-Catholics are smaller than is popularly supposed.

Canfield's procedures, designed to attract leading Catholics, met with modest success, at first with Catholic journalists in the East, and later with some Catholic family life leaders in the Midwest. But Catholic resistance to contraception had not yet in 1962 crumbled. Practically all Catholic spokesmen, including scholars, were still calling contraception a moral evil.

Cass Canfield was not revealing all his approaches to the Catholic community. In production (1962) was a volume which would prove to be a Planned Parenthood *coup de grace.* Dr. John Rock became the author and Christian Herter the endorser of a book (released in 1963) which would stir up real controversy *within the Catholic Church.* The book was skillfully conceived. Its title: *The Time Has Come: A Catholic Doctor's Proposal To End the Battle Over Birth Control.* Herter called Rock's contribution to religious discussion on birth control only slightly less important than his scientific contribution to the discovery of the pill. The publisher, Alfred A. Knopf, praised the special qualifications of John Rock for this role, proposing him "as a dedicated Roman Catholic." Rock was (by virtue of thirty years' direct service) a dedicated Planned Parenthood Federationist and a distinguished Harvard Professor of gynecology, but his Catholic qualifications are not recognized in any edition of the *American Catholic Who's Who* for any of the ten years prior to the publication of *The Time Has Come.* Rock's familiarity with things Catholic became evident, too, when asked at a press conference why the book, if it was Catholic, lacked an imprimatur. Rock replied that he was unaware of this requirement. Dr. Herbert Ratner, Commissioner of Public Health at Oak Park, Illinois, raised serious questions at that late date in Rock's life about the propriety of appending the word "Catholic" to the author's qualifications. Rock's statements justifying abortion (e.g., "embryos have the same responsibility to the preservation of the human race as soldiers") and predictions about the ultimate acceptability of abortion, also, according to Ratner, made the use of the word "Catholic" a misleading promotional aspect for the sale of this book (*Commonweal,* July 5, 1963). When Rock co-authored *Voluntary Parenthood* in 1947 with the Public Information Director of Planned Parenthood, there was no reference to his Catholicity. The reasons for introducing the religious identification in 1963 were compelling from the Federation's public relations perspective.

But Catholic complaints to the contrary, Planned Parenthood's ploy proved to be successful. Rock's book was widely discussed in Catholic circles. While some Catholic critics looked upon it as a piece of Planned Parenthood propaganda, a careful compilation of half-truths about Catholic doctrine, a literary pill to lull unsuspecting Catholics into the reasonableness of the contraceptive cause, Catholics read the book and discussed it. The editors of *Commonweal* (May 17, 1963), though admitting Rock distorted important facts of Catholic life (most Catholic theologians opposed Rock's view on the morality of the pill and opposed his effort to downgrade the Papal doctrine as an "authoritative position binding on Catholics"), thought that the time had come for Catholic theologians to confront the issues Rock raised.

This was precisely what Planned Parenthood hoped would happen. And the new affluent, well-educated middle-class Catholics apparently were ready.

3. The Issues Facing the Catholic Church

The issues which by 1960 began to surface for the Catholic Church were the same issues which faced the Church of England in 1930.

The question uppermost in the minds of many was: Is contraception really intrinsically immoral?

All other matters in the discussion about contraception were side issues.

The debate frequently raged on those side issues. But the core questions about contraception always remained: Was there something in the very nature of the marriage act—a "given" from God—which precluded the moral right of human beings directly and effectively to exclude His purposes while pursuing their own? Was there by divine intent a necessary connection between sexual loving in marriage and God-loving, too, at least to the extent that every sexual union must be open to a child, if so be His will?

The Catholic Church had always said yes.

But in 1960 old questions were raised anew. Catholics who wanted the condemnation lifted would be required to demonstrate that contraception was not intrinsically immoral, that contraceptive use of marriage can be positively virtuous.

This moral theological controversy over contraception factually was only a small argument within a much larger debate exploring more radical ground: Has God commanded anything absolutely? Is there really a divinely established moral order? Are we talking about a real God or man's own primitive myths about "God"? Has God revealed Himself in nature as in Jesus Christ? Who says He has and who decides what He revealed, if He did?

For purposes of separating the later arguments, it is well to understand what the issues were not:

> Condemnation of contraception did not necessarily imply a denigration of sex itself or sexual loving by husband and wife. Loving is an integral part of married life, even when childbearing is unlikely or impossible. Hardship in childbearing or social difficulties in raising a family have nothing to do with the morality or the immorality of a contraceptive marital act.
>
> The intrinsic morality or immorality of any human act is not decided by popular vote. (Obviously the Catholic vote in 1950 was different from what is reported for 1970.)
>
> The conscience of the individual person does not decide the goodness or badness of contraception. At best a person's conscience—if it is a good conscience—declares him sinless or guiltless. He does not judge rightness or wrongness except for himself.
>
> The "pill" is not the issue. Standard Catholic moral doctrine permits therapy, even chemical therapy, for all kinds of disorders. Steroids were

discovered as therapy for disorders before it was realized they also sterilized fertile women while they were being taken. The morality of chemical contraceptives must be decided on the same basis as mechanical devices.

The formal note "infallibility" used or not used in connection with pronouncements of the Church in moral matters is not a central issue to the evaluation of contraception as immoral. The Church teaches many things without fear of error, i.e., with certainty, without explicitly calling the doctrine "infallible," a technical term rarely used and used for special reasons to make clear to the faithful the special solemnity of a particular pronouncement. In other words, if a doctrine is not pronounced "infallible," this does not mean (in English terminology) that it is "fallible"—i.e., likely to be wrong.

The right of dissent is not an issue in determining the morality of contraception, if by that is meant dissenters represent another rule of faith apart from the teaching Church. Catholics may as individuals disagree, deny, disobey (and in that sense "dissent") a Church teaching or ruling, but the fact that dissenting voices exist does not mean that they exist by right, especially if dissenting views have been condemned by the teaching Church.

The subsequent encyclical *Humanae vitae* addressed itself to all the side issues but centered attention first on the central issue of contraception's intrinsic immorality and in a way many Catholics did not like.

4. Contraception Prior to 1965

Almost until 1963 no one conceived that the Catholic Church would ever accept artificial contraception as an approved method of birth control.

From the early days of Christian history the bishops of the Catholic Church all over the world from different cultural settings, together with many Popes, had taught consistently that contraception was wrong, had insisted that Catholic people take that rejection as part of God's law. It is also true that Catholic people understood and accepted the Church's doctrine, even when they departed from its norm, as many frequently did.

But contraception was said to be wrong, was taught to be wrong everywhere in the Church, and the issue appeared closed forever. John T. Noonan's review of the doctrine's history concluded:

> "The teachers of the Church have taught without hesitation or variation that certain acts preventing procreation are gravely sinful. No Catholic theologian has ever taught, 'contraception is a good act.' The teaching on contraception is clear and apparently fixed forever" (*Contraception*, p. 6).

Though at the end of his volume Noonan goes on to question this fixity, the former Notre Dame Law professor was able to make that positive judgment in 1965.

A report prepared for the American bishops in the same year in response to a query from the Holy See concerning the birth control tendencies among American Catholics summarized the state of the questions as follows:

> "American theologians and moralists have not defended in published articles a departure from traditional teaching on birth control. They have unanimously condemned contraception, whether by means of interference with the marriage act or by means of sterilizing operations. Even with regard to the 'pill' American theologians have disapproved its use to prevent conception, apparently, *with practical unanimity* (italics added). Nor is there any tendency in their published writings to defend the idea that the Church will or can change her substantial teaching on birth control."

This paragraph was written during the period in which the professional theologian assigned himself an active but modest role in the teaching Church. In 1962 retiring president Father Aloysius McDonough, C.P., reminded the 17th Annual Convention of CTSA that, while the professional theologian made influential and invaluable contributions to the Church, "in relation to the hierarchy, the position of the theologian in the economy of the Teaching Church is auxiliary, subsidiary." Even Catholic journalist John Cogley admitted to a *New York Times Magazine* audience that those in the Church who rejected the Catholic doctrine were as of June 20, 1965, only a small group.

All American Catholic scholars upheld Catholic doctrine with remarkable unity, so that the faithful experienced no deviance between abstract teaching and Catholic practice, either in the pulpit or the confessional—at least until the latter months of 1964.

In 1960, John L. Thomas, S.J. (*Theological Studies*, Volume 20) specified contraception's particular evil to be the prevention of the marital act from fulfilling its "primary natural purpose." In the December 1961 issue of *Theological Studies*, Joseph J. Farraher, S.J., clearly taught the same. In 1962 Father Enda McDonagh of Maynooth says "the two ends (of marriage) are not separable. They are not even completely distinct" (*Irish Theological Quarterly*, 1962, p. 283). In 1963, Gerald Kelly, S.J., explained to the 18th annual convention of the *Catholic Theological Society of America* why contraception was evil. With colleague John C. Ford in the same year he told why the Church's teaching on birth control will not change (*Catholic World*, November 1963), a conclusion their colleague D. O'Callaghan would reassert with conviction a year later in *The Irish Ecclesiastical Record*, November 1964. Felix F. Cardegna, S.J., in 1964, while expressing the hope that "the Church will again and more strongly condemn all forms of contraception," predicted, too, that "all Catholics are ready to accept the judgment of the Holy See in this matter" (*Theological Studies*, December 1964). On June 15, 1965, Father Richard A. McCormick, S.J., informed the *Cath-*

olic Physicians Guild of Chicago that the Catholic norms on contraception, even for using the pill, were still in force.

One statement of the Catholic case was made in 1963 by Jesuit Moralist Joseph Fuchs, in his little book on the relationship of chastity and sexuality *(De Castitate et Ordine Sexual;* p. 45).

> "The Creator so arranged the sexual act that it is simultaneously both per se generative and per se expressive of intimate oblative love. He has so arranged it that procreation would take place from an act intimately expressive of conjugal love and that this act expressive of conjugal love would tend toward procreation. Therefore, an act which *of itself* does not appear to be apt for procreation is by this very fact shown to be one which does not conform to the intentions of the Creator. The same thing should be said about an act which *of itself* is not apt for the expression of oblative love. Indeed, an act which is not apt for procreation is by this very fact shown to be one which is of itself not apt for the expression of conjugal love; for the sexual act is one."

Fuchs says here that within Christian understanding what God has joined together (the procreative and loving elements of sexual relations in marriage), no man may put asunder. Anything which destroys the essential God-given purpose of life-giving or spouse loving is wrong. Contraception offends the procreative meaning, but other practices—such as artificial insemination, condemned by Pius XII—are also intrinsically evil, although conducive to procreation, because such behavior radically denies the essential love element required for natural, morally good, sexual relations between husband and wife.

Pope Paul VI five years later will say the same thing in other words, but by then Father Fuchs was himself ready to accept contraception.

5. What Went Wrong

Although family life movements in the United States were flourishing and even in 1960 Europe (an auxiliary bishop in Belgium, named Leon Joseph Suenens, began a book *Love and Control* with the assumption that contraception was taboo for Catholics), pressures were being brought to bear on the Church authorities and Catholic faithful designed to soften the Catholic climate considerably.

First, there was the subtle shift within Catholic circles in the stress from having children to responsible parenthood, to restricting family size.

Secondly, the deliberations of the Second Vatican Council itself contributed to a new mood.

The pressure for smaller and smaller Catholic families was considerable. A book like *The Catholic Marriage Manual* sold 250,000 copies from 1958 onward in part because of its positive approach to multi-child families. When a sequel followed in 1963, entitled *Birth Control and Catholics*, reviewer Father John A. O'Brien of Notre Dame observed: "A serious defect [of the latter book] is the overemphasis placed upon the large family" (Ave Maria, November 30, 1963). O'Brien also objected to tying family planning to contraception and sterilization.

Father O'Brien became an early advocate of "responsible parenthood" among Catholics. While not yet endorsing contraception the erstwhile Catholic apologetician's call for responsible parenthood was avidly greeted, not only by Notre Dame's *Ave Maria*, but by such Protestant publications as *Christian Century* and the slick weekly *Look*. On November 21, 1961, Father O'Brien joined such Planned Parenthood advocates as Philip Hauser, William Vogt, William Draper in a symposium of opinion for *Look*, entitled "America's Population Crisis." Hauser was concerned about what population growth was doing to parking and driving in New York City. Vogt asked (in 1961): "Do you think your children have a right to offspring beyond perhaps the second one?" Draper praised post-war Japan for radically cutting its birthrate "by drastic measures such as legalized abortion," which, Draper said, "we would not approve."

This was the rising climate in the immediate pre-Vatican II period for those Catholics discussing birth control publicly. Panelists on TV, usually three or four to one in favor of contraception, sterilization and abortion—always made it appear that the orthodox Catholic was an oddity in American society. In the *Look* piece Father O'Brien followed the Planned Parenthood agenda. His article, entitled "A Priest's View: Let's Take Birth Control Out of Politics," suggested to Catholics that they cease fighting public policy on contraceptive measures. In spite of many state laws (said O'Brien), "the Roman Catholic Church sanctions a much more liberal policy on family planning." Since the Catholic Church had nothing to do with birth control laws on state books, Catholics who fight to retain them are compared by O'Brien to prohibitionists. His final suggestion that Catholics carry their fight about contraception into theological circles but not into the political arena, seems naive and hindsight. The politics of contraception in 1961 became its theology in 1965. Later, permissive politics on abortion would lead to a theological shift on that subject also.

Two years later, Father O'Brien simultaneously published in *Ave Maria* and in *Christian Century* an article entitled "Family Planning in an Exploding Population." A development in O'Brien's thinking has occurred. There is now something intrinsically good about a regulated family. While Winfield Best, Executive Vice President of the Planned Parenthood, praised the article, Msgr. John C. Knott of the Family Life Bureau—N.C.W.C. chides O'Brien for the things he did not say about Catholic family planning:

> "I am afraid he leaves in the minds of both Catholic and Protestant readers that these things (about the legitimacy of regulating births) are all that the Church says. And this is not so. The very

authorities he cites go on to insist in the next breath that the Church does not and will not accept the contraceptive view of married life, which the birth control ideology takes for granted" (*America*, September 7, 1963).

If one Catholic mood countenanced political silence about the spread of contraception, a different temper of popular writing and television appearances dictated attacks by Catholics on the Church doctrine. In *Jubilee* (December, 1963) a man and woman express doubts about the Catholic position. Later on, in the *Saturday Evening Post* (April 10, 1964) the same woman pleads more explicitly for a reversal of traditional doctrine, claiming that the Church "places married Catholics in an impossible position." The crescendo of dissenting Catholics wending their way to television studios became so intense, that when the *American Broadcasting System* wished to balance a series of one-sided pro-contraceptive presentations by televising a panel of religious leaders who opposed contraception, one distinguished Orthodox Jewish scholar refused to participate because he doubted the determination of the Catholic Church to defend the essentials of the Judeao-Christian tradition on contraception.

What made ABC concerned about having an "orthodox" presentation of the issue is symptomatic of how the Church was treated in general by the media. During a dispute in New York City over whether social workers should have authority to dispense birth control counsel to the poor, a Catholic leader was kinescoped in the afternoon saying no one in New York over sixteen was unknowlegeable about where to purchase a contraceptive. When the presentation was made on the evening news, the ABC reporter had in the meantime found a Spanish lady (provided by Planned Parenthood) to say *she* did not know and her priest would not tell her. The reporter later was discharged but anti-Catholic bias of the news stories remained a factor in motioning the Catholic community toward contraception.

Other ancillary factors also helped loosen Catholic loyalties to traditional doctrine. Books like *Contraception and Holiness, Contraception and Catholics, Catholics and Birth Control, Population: Moral and Theological Considerations, The Experience of Marriage, Contraception Versus Tradition* began to receive favorable comment in Catholic magazines. *The National Catholic Reporter*, freed of its Kansas City foundation, became under the editorship of Robert Hoyt a widely read newspaper for priests and religious. NCR devoted featured views favorable to contraception.

The educational machinery of the federal government was another element in popularizing family planning, or at least muting opposition to government involvement in such activity. Catholic bishops in 1959 said they would not support publicly financed programs of this kind, but four years later 53 per cent of American Catholics were reported by Gallup as favoring governmental dispensation of information on birth control. By 1965, when 78 per cent of Catholics had moved to the affirmative side of the question, federal involvement in birth control programs was on the upswing. The first grant of federal funds had already been made by the *Office of Economic Opportunity* to Corpus Christi, Texas, for a community birth control program. Through the *Public Health Service*, many projects related to birth control were already under way.

On January 4, 1965, in a carefully worded sentence, the newly re-elected President Lyndon B. Johnson told Congress in his State of the Union message: "I will seek new ways to use our knowledge to help deal with the explosion in world population and the growing scarcity in world resources." This was the first time in the nation's history that a President gave official sanction to government efforts in this area.

Congress was not idle either. Senator Ernest F. Gruening of Alaska, a long-time advocate of Planned Parenthood, introduced a family planning bill into the Senate. Feeling that his greatest contribution to the cause was to turn Senate hearings into a public platform, Gruening first called those witnesses who could glamorize the principles of his bill. When Gruening questioned John Rock, he raised possible changes in Catholic teaching and about the "immorality" of the social conditions which grew out of the absence of birth control. *The New York Times* and the *Washington Post* gave extensive coverage to these hearings, as did the Huntley-Brinkley report on TV. In the meantime *National Educational Television*, financed in part by government money, prepared a series of six films on the population crises of Brazil, Europe, Japan, India, and the United States. Filming took place in every part of the world and a panel of demographers contributed to their production. The last film dealt with the medical aspects of family planning.

The full impact on Catholics of this contraceptive promotion during 1963-1965 was not yet measurable. Catholic partisans of contraception usually shied away from endorsing the wrong methods publicly. But they talked repeatedly about liberal public policy, about civil freedom for the non-Catholic conscience, for responsible parenthood by Catholics. Later, the effect of this quiet approach was noticeable. Father John A. O'Brien, for example, who never previously endorsed contraception, published almost simultaneously with *Humanae vitae* a new book, *Family Planning in an Exploding Population* with three distinctive features: (1) The book was dedicated to President Lyndon B. Johnson, John D. Rockefeller III, and Senator Ernest F. Gruening; (2) contained an insert citing Catholic University professors who publicly dissented from *Humanae vitae*; and (3) the last two paragraphs pleaded with the Pope to let Catholics use contraceptives.

6. The Second Vatican Council

Many people blame the Council itself for the ultimate confusion of the Catholic faithful. Others trace dissent from Catholic doctrine to false allegations about what the Council said about marriage and family life.

Before recalling the dynamic confrontations between Catholic Fathers over Vatican II's final document *(Pastoral Constitution on the Church in the Modern World—Gaudium et Spes)* it is important to summarize the Council's final decisions on this controverted subject:

1. "God Himself is the author of marriage and has endowed it with various benefits and with various ends in view" (no. 48).

2. "By its very nature the institution of marriage and married love is ordered to the procreation and education of the offspring" (no. 48).

3. "It is imperative to give suitable and timely instruction to young people—about the dignity of married love" (no. 49).

4. "Without intending to underestimate the other ends of marriage, it must be said that the true married love and the whole structure of family life which results from it is directed to disposing the spouses to cooperate valiantly with the love of the Creator and Savior, who through them will increase and enrich His family from day to day" (no. 50).

5. "It is the married couples themselves who must in the last analysis arrive at these judgments before God" (no. 50).

6. "Among the married couples who thus fulfill their God-given message, special mention should be made of those who after prudent reflection and common decision courageously undertake the proper upbringing of a large number of children" (no. 50).

7. "When it is a question of harmonizing married love with the responsible transmission of life, it is not enough to take only the good intention and the evaluation of motives into account; the objective criteria must be used, criteria drawn from the nature of the human person, criteria which respect the total meaning of mutual self-giving and human procreation in the context of true love" (no. 51).

8. "In questions of birth regulation the sons of the Church, faithful to those principles, are forbidden to use methods disapproved of by the teaching

authority of the Church in its interpretation of the divine law" (no. 51). Here follows famous footnote 14 which refers to statements of Pius XI, Piux XII, Paul VI, upholding the ban on contraception and a reminder also that Paul VI had reserved certain birth control questions to himself. The last line of the footnote has been used to "prove" the Council's intended ambiguity. It reads: "With the doctrine of the magisterium in this state, this Holy Synod does not intend to propose immediately concrete solutions."

Gaudium et Spes attempted to reconcile the personalist values symbolized in the expression "married love" without downgrading its relationship to childbearing, even the bearing of many children. The positive endorsement of private judgment in matters of birth regulation is balanced by the reminder that objective as well as subjective norms of morality govern decision making, with the special reminder that "methods disapproved of by the teaching authority of the Church were forbidden." All this seems clear in the final texts.

But all was not so crystal clear in the conciliar debates and the jockeying over the terminology to be used, especially as the disagreements were related to the general public by media representatives already committed to the proposition that the Catholic Church must change, will change.

First, the jockeying over terminology. The preliminary text of the section on marriage (May 16, 1965) was vague on contraception and a second schemata (November 16, 1965) was drafted to include a reference to objective moral criteria and contraception. Omitted at that time, however, was any reference to previous papal statements on the subject. Some parties to the drafting preferred the document remain as it was; others sought to limit the possibility of loose interpretation of the Council's meaning *after* the bishops went home by having contraception specifically mentioned. The fear that silence in the text would be taken to suggest a Church backing away from its historic condemnation of contraception was not small. Prior to submission for final approval, the Council Fathers tightened the proposed schema.

On November 23, 1965, the Pope instructed the Secretary of State to inform the Council's *Theological Commission* that he wanted the final text to contain clear and open references to Pius XI's *Casti connubii* (1930) and Pius XII's *Allocution to Midwives* (1951) both of which condemned contraception. The Commission added these references and also Pope Paul's own statement of June 23, 1964. ("They [the norms given by Pius XII] should, therefore, be regarded as valid, at least as long as we do not consider ourselves obliged in conscience to modify them."), with its advisory that the Pope was reserving certain questions to himself. This turned out to be one of the strongest interventions of Pope Paul during the Council but proved to be only partially effective.

The intervention was looked upon by contraception-minded *periti* as a blow to their efforts to place the Church behind a doctrinal statement which effectively granted couples the right to choose conjugal love over children (without regard to the means of birth control). The Pope's intervention, though private, made front page news in next morning's Roman papers implying in its text that a showdown of conciliar forces was in the making. The move to strengthen the text against contraception was interpreted as a strike at the independence of the Council. Bishops were quoted as resenting being "bulldozed" by the Pope. But the Pope responded that, while not choosy about *how* the Council took up his demands (with his permission some accommodations on the actual formulations were reached), he wanted no tampering with Catholic doctrine in the Council text (Xavier Rynne, *The Fourth Session*, pp. 211-224). Whether the Pope was as firm as he has been reported is a matter of dispute.

Prior to the vote, the Council Fathers heard explained that the submitted text was intended in no. 47 to condemn "illicit practices against generation," called "unlawful contraceptive practices" in the Flannery translation. (Some use this explanation to suggest that the Council was implying that there were "lawful" contraceptive practices. It was amid this confusion that the schema was brought to a vote on December 4, 1965, and passed. (A strange thing occurred two days before the vote. The printed text given to the bishops lacked the exact page reference to *Casti connubii's* specific condemnation. The Holy Father himself had this omission called to public attention and the page reference reinserted in the promulgated document.)

Footnote 14 later was to be used to "prove" that all questions on contraception were still open, that the Pope allowed the footnote to say so. (See John L. Thomas, S.J., *America*, February 2, 1966, and the response of John C. Ford, S.J., *America*, April 16, 1966). However, the publication of *Humanae vitae* illegitimizes such an interpretation. The only open question on June 23, 1964 was the relation of the "pill" to Catholic doctrine, not the doctrine itself. Those who read otherwise tried to establish a linguistic case, but clearly they did not read Pope Paul's mind correctly. (They claim, however, the correctness of their reading of the Council's mind. But there was no single conciliar mind to which anyone can refer on this matter—because the accepted formulas are ambiguous.)

During the same pre-*Humanae vitae* period another justification of contraception appeared in Catholic journals; viz., single married acts need not be procreative, if the entire marriage was. This defense of contraception was based on the allegation that the Council equated marital love with intercourse, that married love without intercourse is not a love of husband and wife in the conciliar sense, that contraceptive intercourse can be a real marital act. The Council did not say so, but Catholic readers were told it did. (See Father Theodore Mackin's article "Vatican II, Contraception and Christian Marriage," *America*, July 15, 1967.) Following 1965 the pro-contraceptive Catholic literature became voluminous.

Regarding the conciliar debates themselves, certain bishops were clearly counted among the pro-contraceptionists. Bernard Cardinal Alfrink representing the Dutch hierarchy, made the method of choice a matter of conflict of duties and private conscience supreme. Cardinal Leger of Canada and Cardinal Suenens of Belgium were quoted at length on the need of doctrinal re-examination and reformulation. Bishop Reuss of Mainz without equivocation was a contraceptionist (and a member of the Birth Control Commission). All these prelates were quoted at length in the press and in articles, while outside of official documents there was little extended or sympathetic treatment of traditional views held by Cardinal Ottaviani, Ruffini and Browne. John Cardinal Heenan for the British bishops tried to end the debate in England (as he said "once and for all" by declaring that for the Council Fathers "contraception is not an open question." Heenan was contradicted by Father Bernard Haring, C.S.S.R. who thought that "the British bishops erred" (*Newsweek*, May 25, 1964). Häring, a member of the Birth Control Commission, in advance of any decision by Pope or Council, was pushing the "pill." During lulls in Council deliberations, he conducted workshops in the United States, mostly in the Midwest, where with the help of Father John A. O'Brien of Notre Dame and Father Walter Imbiorski, director of Chicago's Cana Conference activity, he insinuated the advisability of married couples making up their own minds on the matter. The year was 1964 and Pope Paul had already said Catholic norms are still in force, but in such a gentle way that insinuating future change did not seem unreasonable. Häring in an interview with Father O'Brien, first passed around in mimeographed form and later published in the *Homiletic and Pastoral Review* (July 1964), stressed this possibility of doctrinal reformulation, thought the Church could change on parenthood as it had on usury (this was not true even in 1964), belabored the catastrophe of four children in four years, categorized as rigorism any position "which forbids almost all tenderness to those couples who do not wish a new pregnancy [and which] is responsible for many broken homes and broken hearts," leaving the final impression that sexual sins need not be looked upon as mortal, i.e., serious.

While Häring was more discreet in his 1964 formulations than later, his "message" of tolerance of methods of birth regulation other than periodic continence encouraged partisans of contraception in South Bend and Chicago. At the 29th National Catholic Family Life Convention in Washington, D.C. (June 25, 1964)—whose theme was "The Rights of Children"—the pressure was strong on delegates to open up the convention to a discussion of contraception, though this effort did not succeed.

Following the close of the Council the pressures increased. Pope Paul tried to stem the tide by repudiating the idea that the Church was in doubt about contraception (October 29, 1966). But a publicly noticed shift came (*Theological Studies*, December, 1966) when Richard McCormick concluded his treatment of contraception indicating how easy it was to sympathize with the view that "one might still be tempted to wonder, notwithstanding contrary opinions, whether the existing laws on contraception are the object of a purely theoretical doubt, which is admitted by all, or whether a practical doubt—ultimately freeing conscience—may legitimately be posited." In June 1967 his confrere Robert H. Springer, S.J., writing in the same journal, said the traditional Catholic teaching already had been modified by Vatican II, thus making future realignment necessary. The *Dutch Catechism* (published also in 1967), representing the Dutch hierarchy, declared (p. 403) that in spite of Vatican II's cautionary against immoral methods, "the last word lies with conscience," not with doctor or confessor. *America* magazine, which under the editorship of Thurston Davis valiantly fought contraceptionists, on September 30, 1967 under the direction of sociologist Donald Campion, S.J., called upon the first Synod of Bishops meeting in Rome to sanction "the use of contraception for the achievement of a truly Christian marriage." When Richard McCormick decided (*Theological Studies*, June 1967, pp. 799-800) that Pope Paul's earlier repudiation of doubt (October 29, 1966) was not enough, ("Only an authentic teaching statement is capable of dissipating genuine doctrinal doubt."), the tide had turned. The authentic teaching statement was to come a year later, but by then the doubters were not inclined to listen.

7. The Papal
Birth Control Commission

The Papal Birth Control Commission, if it was planned only as a "pill commission," certainly ended accomplishing little good for the Church. The Commission began as a study of steroids that in view of *Humanae vitae* served the practical purpose of sowing division within the Church over issues other than contraception. In hindsight, it would have been better to let the bishops argue about contraception on the Council floor, thus finishing the matter once and for all, than to allow an ever expanding group of experts to feed doubts into local arenas throughout the Catholic world, and insulting statements about the rectitude of the traditional Catholic position. *Humanae vitae* has ratified the Catholic teaching on contraception as a matter of God-given moral law. A century from now—when natural family planning may be commonly used as the means of regulating family size—intellectuals, presently enamored of chemical and surgical warfare on the human body—may take note of the Church's courage in sticking to its principles under heavy fire. But in 1964-1965 Pope Paul, who through the *National Catholic Welfare Conference* canvassed the bishops of the world on contraception (as Pius XII did prior to declaring Mary's Assumption), knew precisely where bishops stood on this doctrine. (Of the American bishops responding to the questionnaire distributed through the *National Catholic Welfare Conference*, only one or two favored modification of the doctrine.) Characteristically, Pope Paul VI, cautious administrator of the Church that he is, inclined to the belief that public discussion of this emotionally packed issue by bishops might prove scandalous and upsetting to the Catholic faithful, so reserved this matter to himself. Critics still downgrade *Humanae vitae* because it was not the collegial decision of the Council, rather than of the Pope *solo cum solo*. The truth is, however (short of an outright public vote) that the birth control encyclical followed more discussion with bishops (and their private vote locally) than any other similar papal decision in the history of the Church. The trouble for the Church originated with the four year delay between consultation and decision. The Pope took a powder keg off the floor of the Aula and stored it in the basement of the Vatican with a long fuse, then seemingly forgot that fuses can be ignited unintentionally. During the period of study, the Pope afforded contraceptionists the time they needed to raise questions about artificial devices, and questions, too, whether the Church's understanding of marriage was correct, whether God had anything much to say about marriage at all, especially about having or not having babies, whether it was within the province of the Church to bind consciences on such personal matters, whether the Church could give more than advice, and whether the Papacy itself had not become an outdated autocracy which should be tailored to proper, if not primitive, size.

The creation and management of the Birth Control Commission was an example of how not to organize a scientific study group. The questions to be studied were never defined. The members were not instructed in the procedures to be used in doing their work. Had the questions been precise and the members required to submit briefs in support of specific answers, votes would have been as unimportant as the number of lawyers pleading before a court. Only arguments would count. The meetings of the Commission did not provide for genuine debate and cross-examination, so that preponderance of people rather than argument, became a major factor in determining "rightness." High Church authorities were interested in answers to questions but the method they chose to get them was hardly rigorous. They did not even appreciate the role the media would play, or how the media would be used by Commission members, in disseminating pro-contraceptive views to the faithful. As well-known priests (and bishops) began to disagree with each other, laity followed priests of their choice. As months of study passed into years, the opinion was circulated that the Pope was looking for a face-saving device before altering the Catholic position. Expectancy of change became practical doubt for many Catholics.

The historical record shows, of course, that the guessers were wrong and the conservative minority, which said that the Church would not change its doctrinal position, were right. Both in the record of the Council and thereafter there was evidence that the Pope's only uncertainty concerned the morality of the pill. Was it capable really of regulating women's monthly cycles so that natural family planning would become more secure? Were Enovid and Ortho-Novum sterilizing agents or abortofacients, rather than contraceptives? What were the long-range medical effects of fooling with a woman's pituitary gland? Dr. John Rock and Planned Parenthood had huckstered the pill as a soporific to Catholic family planners. Indeed, advertisements suggested that pill-taking was just another form of natural family planning. European theologians like Father Louis Janssens and Father Bernard Häring swallowed the pill as an antidote to the Catholic birth control problem. The first birth control commission did not agree on the pill, and the second quickly began to understand (what is even clearer in 1978 than in 1965) that the pill was medically dangerous for long term use. Theologians continued to argue about the conditions under which the pill could be morally acceptable, as the Pope's medical advisers wrote it off as the universal answer to the birth-control problem.

About the time this conclusion was reached, the focus of attention turned to any and all kinds of contraception and to the Church's basic and historic position.

This change was also unanticipated by Church authority. While morning vision is always clearer, a commission composed of sociologists, economists, biologists, theologians, parish priests, married couples, statisticians—57 in all—would tend to be empirical rather than doctrinal and divided in their opinions. A social scientist could only say that contraception works or does not, that people want this method or that, or none. Once the world of doctrine was left behind, no scientist, no married couple, no individual priest could demonstrate with certitude a moral position on any subject. Apart from doctrine, a private reading, a common reading or an official Church reading would prevail at the same time for different audiences. Using the tools of science or sophisticated logic cannot guarantee conviction that contraception (or abortion or divorce, etc.) is right, wrong, always or sometimes. A private reading satisfies many religionists and humanists; a common reading is helpful to the determination of public policy in a Democratic society; but a Catholic Church reading was bound to be based on the 2,000 year teaching as an interpretation of God's law.

There are other questions which can be raised about the Commission. Granted that it represented an honest effort to explore new scientific developments, why was not membership confined to scientists who were experts about such things and theologians who were professionally qualified to evaluate new discoveries against the Church's insistence that their use be governed by the *objective* requirements of the moral law? The Commission then would have been "scientific," less moved by subjective feelings, factual states, or by political forces. Subjective feelings and factual states were worth knowing, population statistics and the extent of resistance to Church doctrine also needed knowing (even·though the reported resistance was found mostly in the better economically situated Catholics of the West). But these data contributed nothing to determining the morality of contraception. Rome knew this from the time the secretary of the Second Commission began to propose members and to determine the Commission's agenda. Father Henri de Reidmatten, O.P., the son of a diplomatic European family, has been variously criticized since for the makeup of the commission and the agenda, yet he was Rome's choice for secretary. If, at the final session of the Pope's Commission, Reidmatten was observed standing, clapping, and cheering the vote which put the majority on the side of contraception, the question earlier might have been asked: Will he balance the interests of the Holy See against his own preferences and/or political pressure? On March 9, 1965, immediately prior to the first Roman meeting Reidmatten was forwarding to commission members the work of John Noonan (American) and Canon de Locht (Belgian), both of whom were pro-contraceptionists. The first formal session of the theological section of the Commission began with an exposition by Noonan, whose chief thrust suggested that the Church's condemnation of contraception was an historically conditioned response to protect the value of infant life itself. If that value could be protected nowadays in other ways, the continued condemnation of contraception might not be necessary. De Locht, while no fan of contraception, had argued a year earlier that for many people contraception was better than nothing.

Almost from the start, therefore, the trend of the commission's labor was toward opening up the entire issue. Noonan, for example, set one framework for the debate by asserting that the Church's ancient doctrine on contraception was merely an ancient response to attacks on sexuality, marriage and childbearing from Stoics, Gnostics, Manicheans, and the like. The one-time Notre Dame scholar gave little emphasis to the fact that early Christian thinkers more likely reflected their Jewish ethical background (which in orthodox circles was always critical of most circumstances surrounding contraception) rather than the need to answer pagans or heretics. The Christian heritage of anti-contraceptionism was not, therefore, an accident of time and place, but derived from a common understanding of the relationship of marriage to parenthood which went back to the Jewish patriarchs and was consistently restated by Church Fathers. Even the repeated use of Onan's sin (Gn. 38:9-10) as a scriptural base for the Catholic doctrine (in spite of modern research which makes his sin merely the refusal to have children by his brother's wife, not spilling his seed) tells what the Church was teaching about contraceptive intercourse. The fact that Orthodox Jews and Protestant Christians factually held to this interpretation until recent times only confirms the traditional reading of Genesis 38, regardless of its acceptance by modern scholars. (No one, however, should concede infallibility to the newer interpretation, which possibly may have grown out of a modern scholarly attempt to undercut the anti-contraceptive interpretation of Onan's sin.)

Another dubious device of Noonan (which has been used by pro-contraceptive debaters, notably Father Häring) is the argument that, since the Church after consistently and solemnly condemning usury for centuries, later found ways to justify interest-taking, so the Church can find ways to justify contraception. But factually, the teaching of the Church on usury (taking money on a loan without some extrinsic title) has not changed. Usury in that sense is still condemned. Furthermore, the Church's teaching on usury was never proclaimed as long, as consistently, as universally, or as solemnly as the Church's teaching on contraception reflected in *Casti Connubii*. The proper comparison to the usury case would be the development of approval for "periodic continence," once science discovered the existence of fertile and infertile periods in women.

Once, however, relativism entered the Commission's deliberations, it should have been seen as a foregone conclusion that absolute principles could not be maintained. Without an absolute anchor moral judgments necessarily follow subjective determination. As early as December, 1962, the *Hugh Moore Foundation* (a Planned Parenthood sponsored organization) distributed "An Appeal to the Vatican" by Dr. Suzanne Le-Soeur Chapelle, a French mother of five and a gynecologist, which spoke of "the immense cry of distress from innumerable homes, torn between their faith and parental duties." She considered "it impossible that the paternal goodness of the Holy Father will not be able to bring a solution to this destructive problem." Not only did an official of the Holy Office (M. Leclerq) assure her that "the decision of the (forthcoming) Council will certainly be sought," but after her visit to Archbishop Jean Levillain, he expressed his sincere "wishes that the problem of birth regulation may be reconsidered from top to bottom."

Soliciting these opinions became a function of the birth control commission. Reidmatten (prior to the 1965 Roman meeting) sent questionnaires around the world seeking to discover, among other things, the acceptability among Catholics of the various methods of regulation and the methods also which ran "the greatest risk of hindering the couple's emotional maturity." In the United States the *Christian Family Movement* became the instrument of distribution. As might be expected, the "horror stories" justifying contraception were many. One of the better and early accounts of what went on in the Pope's birth control commission was published in the *Ladies' Home Journal* for March, 1966. The opening paragraphs contain the following poignant lines:

> "Emotionally and psychologically the rhythm method has been harmful to our marriage. Our love, which is continually deepening in Christ and in each other, must, of its nature, seek union. This union is almost continually denied, and the frustration is great....
>
> "Ten children in twelve years—it hardly seems as if it works. After a complete nervous breakdown and an attempted suicide, we have nothing left to do but abstain."

Quoting the summary of responses to the Holy See, the article continues:

> "They represent so much anguish and suffer-
> ing. When there is this much widespread unhap-
> piness, this much that is destructive of the very
> ideals of marriage the Church wants to preserve,
> something is wrong."

Drawing on what could only be inside information
intended to deprecate the traditional Catholic view of
marriage, Lois R. Chevalier, the author, made this
reference to what only could have been the presentation
to the Commission by Dr. and Madame Rendu, France's
equivalent of America's CFM: "The French are wild.
They have a full-blown mystique about sex and love.
Their expositions were poetry and prose: absolutely in-
comprehensible to an Anglo-Saxon." The Rendus talked
with Commission members about sex within the context
of Christian married love and the beauty of marital
chastity for perfecting true married love.

John and Eileen Farrell, formerly of Chicago's Cana
Conference, were dubious from the beginning about
what the Commission's questionnaire might elicit beyond
the pressing urgency of contraception for aggrieved
couples. Questionnaires like prophecies often contribute
to their fulfillment. The Farrells raised the central question which the questionnaire raised in their minds.

> "It is hoped that the questionnaire does not
> represent the mentality of the [birth control] Com-
> mission but is somehow intended to stimulate
> discussion leading to a clearer understanding of the
> Church's consistent teaching. There seems to be no
> other explanation for initiating an inquiry about
> contraceptive methods with no mention of the basic
> issue which is the natural and supernatural value of
> children."

On reading the questionnaire from Rome closely, the
Farrells found it also inconceivable that in the Papal
Commission's list of subject matters "no mention is made
of continence or mortification." Neither did they like the
questionnaire's assumption of an ongoing high rate of
"fertility which does not exist," nor "the tone of many

questions [which] suggests that family planning is a foregone conclusion." In providing their view of the world to come, the Farrells prophesied (January, 1965) that "sterilization is the family planning method of tomorrow," and suggested at the same time (what would later be a concern of Pope Paul) that a close look at the correlation of contraception and sexual promiscuity among the young should be taken.

These views, however, did not compete on equal terms with the humanist concerns of the growing majority, nor with the natural sympathy for the burdens sometimes placed on fertile married couples, advancing in age and already fruitful. The Holland Dutch representative offered existentialist arguments and several German spokesmen also leaned in that direction. World War II cruelties had radically touched both Dutch and German intellectuals. Dutch Catholicism in particular, which once was rigid and separatist (bishops there frequently told politicians how to vote, Catholics and Protestants were highly ghettoized), developed in the post-war era a passionate desire to break down barriers with other religionists. One professor from the Catholic University of Nijmegen explained: "When you share bunkers and churches with fellow countrymen of all persuasions under a cascade of bombs sent by an unbelieving madman, religious differences do not seem to count for much."

African and Indian commission members viewed birth control differently. Africans respected large families. One of the best defenders of natural family planning came from India. For those who were interested, a highly successful government plan of natural family planning on the African coastline island *Mauritius* (mostly non-Catholic) was brought to the attention of the delegates.

In the end, however, the influence of the mid-European intellectuals prevailed, with some solid help from the American delegation whose majority had gone contraceptionist. The Americans were encouraged also by what was going on at home, such as the statement prepared by thirty-seven Catholic academicians meeting in conference at Notre Dame. The Notre Dame group concluded that old Catholic norms are no longer operative because they do not reflect "the complexity and the inherent value of sexuality in human life."

Sharp division among commission members was taken by some to mean that the "Church's mind" was not settled on the subject. Michael Novak thought the obstacle to Catholic acceptance of contraception was "emotional, not theological" (Newsweek, April 12, 1965). Charles Davis writing later in the Clergy Review (December, 1966) asserted "the Church is in danger of losing its soul to save its face." All the while the Pope kept studying the question. John Noonan sympathized with the Pope: "In a matter of such great importance to millions of persons, born and to be born, he believes he cannot discharge his office by accepting the report of experts. He, himself, must know and judge personally. This is the decision not of a callous but a conscientious man. Its honesty requires respect" (Commonweal, February 17, 1967).

But someone soon decided that the Pope's conscientiousness and honesty needed nudging, so they leaked the drafts of both majority and minority conclusions of the Papal Birth Control Commission to the National Catholic Reporter. The story made front page news everywhere on April 17, 1967. The squeeze on the Pope was real.

Commonweal editorialists told its readership (April 28, 1967) what the commission drafts meant to them:

> "For better or worse, the debate over birth control in the Church has served as a focal point for all manner of issues far more basic than the morality of contraception. Among these have been the nature of marriage, the man-woman relationship, the role and value of the Church's teaching authority, the place of the free conscience in the Church, the validity of natural law, the nature of morality and the Church's witness to the world."

These certainly were the fundamental issues which would continue to be argued in the press, in classrooms and parish halls of the Church throughout the ensuing fifteen months. While change-makers had the Catholic faithful fired up for the Church's acceptance of contraception, apparently at the highest level of the Church no one gave consideration to counter-efforts of education to prepare Mass-goers for *Humanae vitae*. This proved to be a disastrous error in judgment.

8. *Humanae Vitae*

On July 25, 1968, Pope Paul issued his now much abused encyclical *Humanae vitae*. Though dealing with the transmission of human life, as its title indicated, the *United States Catholic Conference* published its contents under the title "The Regulation of Birth." This is what interested the Western world, even if that was not what the encyclical was *all* about.

No papal pronouncement was ever greeted with such hostility from its own. Up to the moment of publication the Catholic converts to contraception thought their fight was ended. A special eleven page report for *U.S. Catholic* on the status of the birth control question, issued one month before (June 1968), concluded that the traditional Catholic law was in doubt and no longer applied. On the secular front, *Time* magazine began on June 21st to publish what would be the first of six articles in three months on Catholic birth control. One week before July 25th, family life pioneer John L. Thomas, S.J., predicted for an Omaha audience Catholic Church approval of medically acceptable birth control methods, other than sterilization (*NCR*, July 24, 1968).

And then the Pope dropped a population bomb of his own. Important sentences (nos. 11-12) of *Humanae vitae* read as follows:

"The Church calling men back to the observance of the norms of the natural law, as interpreted by their constant doctrine, teaches that each and every marriage act must remain open to the transmission of life.

"That teaching, often set forth by the magisterium, is founded upon the inseparable connection, willed by God and unable to be broken by man on his own initiative, between the two meanings of the conjugal act: The unitive meaning and the procreative meaning."

In section 14 the Pope goes on to outline the Catholic doctrine on "illicit ways of regulating birth," saying, "We must once again declare that the direct interruption of the generative process already begun, and, above all, directly willed and procured abortion, even if for therapeutic reasons, are to be absolutely excluded as licit means of regulating birth." The Pope warned (no. 17) about the grave consequences of desacralizing marriage in this manner and the social consequences of contraception.

These specific references to contraception and its rejection by the Pope do not stand alone. They must be seen within the context of his entire teaching, which can be summarized as follows:

1. On Human Life

The encyclical *Humanae vitae* is a sharp reminder that human life is unique. Every human being who comes into existence is a person the exact like of whom the world has never seen before and will never see again, someone whom God Himself wants to exist with Him for all eternity, an individual with a capacity to reach out beyond himself and help build new worlds and transform this one. Because of this, the act that brings him into existence involves cooperation by two human beings with the creative power of God, who alone can bring this immortal person into existence—and this act of procreation acquires a sacredness which may never be denied.

This is why the Church has always been so concerned with human life, why she has opposed abortion and euthanasia, why she has taken care even of infants born so malformed that they will never reach full mental maturity in this life. It is why her social doctrine has been so concerned, over the last century, to help men live in the conditions that are worthy of their human dignity. It is why she is concerned with peace at a time when modern weapons of war can wipe out human lives on a scale undreamed of in the past.

Humanae vitae recalls men to a deeper recognition of the importance of human life and ways that God has provided for human beings to share in bestowing it on others.

2. On Sex

The encyclical *Humanae vitae* is a sharp reminder that sex is sacred in God's eyes—something that may not be cut off from its proper relationship to the origin of human life. This does not mean that sex has no other important roles to play—as a concrete experience of the marriage bond's unity, as something joyful and enjoyable, as a celebration of human life itself. But it does mean that sex loses its truest and most profound meaning in God's plan if it is separated from its necessary relationship to the origins of life. The evidence of where this kind of separation leads is all around: a flood of pornography that would have been inconceivable 15 years ago, a commercialization of sex in stage and film productions that leaves nothing sacred, a casual acceptance of promiscuity in varying degrees, a so-called sexual revolution in the matter of pre-marital relationships, a tendency to disregard any moral implication in homosexuality.

Humanae vitae recalls us to a deeper acknowledgement of the sacredness and the beauty of sex, because God created sex to enable men to cooperate with Him in the greatest of all natural acts and powers—bringing a new person into the world.

3. On Absolute Principles

The encyclical *Humanae vitae* is a sharp reminder that, in a world of shifting values, there are still principles that hold now as in the past—in all places and circumstances—and that will still hold true on the day when God calls the whole of the human race to be happy with Him forever. Many things which were once worthwhile no longer are so. The modern world encourages use and comfort and enjoyment of the good life, holds out promise of greater goods to come—and in this sense has positive value. But good values can be dismissed with worn-out customs. Ease and comfort can lead men to give up what they believe in. The promise of a better life can lead us to forget moral responsibilities in the present.

Humanae vitae reminds men that God wants the law of the Lord obeyed, that what seems to be easiest is not always best, that God's grace enables us to live up to His norms even when it requires great effort.

4. On the Supernatural

The encyclical *Humanae vitae* is also a reminder that the Holy Spirit is real in the life of a Christian and at work in our own day. In asking for acceptance of what the Church had always taught in this matter, the Holy Father appeals to the promise of assistance from the Holy Spirit made to Peter and the apostles and through them to Pope and bishops. Pope Paul knew that if the arguments were so clear in either direction as to exclude all doubt, there would never have been a wait of four years for a final answer. But he also knew that the Holy Spirit, who had been with the Church in harder days than these, would not fail to provide the direction that was needed.

Also, the Pontiff knew that Catholics, whose lives are built on faith in things that are not fully seen, would realize that God's plan was at work even in those cases where contraception would seem from a human point of view to offer a simpler solution. Someone looking at a consecrated host without the eyes of faith misses the true reality that is there; someone speaking to Jesus as He walked the street of Nazareth would never, on his own, recognize that this man was God; someone beholding an infant fresh from the baptismal font doesn't see the life of God within him; those who looked at a man suffering on a cross 2,000 years ago did not see Redemption. But the eyes of faith and the virtues of trust, and our love of God, who loves us more than we love Him, even when He asks hard things of us, assure us that God's ways are the best ways, in this as in all other things.

Humanae vitae reminds men to look beyond the surface view of things to the divine truth beneath.

5. On Involvement With Others

The encyclical *Humanae vitae* is a sharp reminder that every Christian must be concerned with the problems of every other human being. The teaching of the encyclical makes hard demands on some people. It is not enough for bishops, priests or laity to consider this someone else's problem. If there is something that Catholics can do—to solve problems or relieve them, with better medical information, or economic aid, with spiritual guidance and support of the sacraments—with sympathy and concern in cases where there is no simple answer, this must be done.

Humanae vitae reminds men of the obligation imposed by Christian love.

9. Immediate Response to *Humanae Vitae*

Probably the most harmful response to *Humanae vitae* came in Rome itself from the man entrusted by the Holy See to release the encyclical to the world's press. Msgr. Fernando Lambruschini, a professor at the Lateran University and a member of the Birth Control Commission who in the end voted with the majority. The rationale for selecting this particular man to be press secretary for the Pope on this subject defies understanding. Lambruschini in the press conference literally undercut any possibility that *Humanae vitae* would tip the scale back toward Catholic doctrine, by telling the press—not once, but twice that the encyclical was *not an infallible pronouncement* (*Catholic Mind*, September 1968).

Not only was this an invitation for continuing debate on an issue the Pope thought he was closing, it also was to suggest to Richard McCormick seven years later the very ongoing debate about contraception, not the Pope's words, were the clear sign of God's will (*The Tablet* [London] February 7, 1975). That was precisely the assumption pro-contraceptionists wished to use as justification for their vigorous dissent.

That public acceptance of the encyclical did not follow should surprise no one. Charles Curran and 51 Washington priests gained notoriety over their rejection. But all over the United States priests and theologians followed Lambruschini's lead. Five days after issuance (July 30, 1968), Fordham University sponsored a panel discussion for 2,000 ready listeners and reporters for the *New York Times*, *Newsweek*, *Time*, and the *Religious News Service* too. The panel was stacked against the Pope. The one priest of five, cast in the role of "Pope's man," is quoted as giving only a "qualified defense" of the encyclical (*America*, August 17, 1968). *America* itself, in the same issue, justified continued dissent in the Church and the use of contraceptives by Catholics, noting that Lambruschini, "as official spokesman in Rome for the encyclical," hinted a possible future and radical change. James T. Burtchaell, at that time chairman of Notre Dame's Theology Department, called for "conscientious resistance," in part on the principle that the Pope's responsibility must be recalled "to more conscionable limits," in part because "practically the only spokesman to support the encyclical vocally are men whose careers depend on ecclesiastical preferment" (*Commonweal*, November 15, 1968). John Cogley asked: "Why not say that the Anglican and Protestant Churches were more correct in their ecclesiology, their moral teachings, and their faithfulness to the spirit of the Gospel than the Church of Rome, which for so long made the kind of claim its own best theologians are now rejecting? If, for example, the Anglicans were right about contraception all along and the Romans were wrong, who are the surer moral teachers? (*Commonweal*, October 11, 1968) Bishop James Shannon of St. Paul told the Holy Father (September 23, 1968) that his "rigid teaching is simply impossible of observance" (*NCR*, June 6, 1969).

And so the dissent continued down to the low levels of the Church, prompting the *Christian Science Monitor* to editorialize (October 11, 1968): *Birth Control Wins.* The Protestant newspaper, citing a Notre Dame study showing that 95 percent of assistant pastors under 30 favored contraception, predicted that "nothing on the face of the earth can stem or reverse" the rejection.

The Pope appeared very much like a defeated man.

10. Catholic War on the Potomac

While dissenters worldwide began to follow identical patterns of resistance, the Pope, facing this opposition, built a few defenses of his own. Within a month of his pronouncement on birth control Paul VI was on his way to Bogotá, Colombia, for the Latin American Bishops' Assembly. He decided once more to confront his critics with the reminder of who they were and who he is.

Among the remarks which received scant attention in the United States were the following:

> "Unfortunately among us some theologians are not on the right path....
> "Some have recourse to ambiguous doctrinal expression and others arrogate to themselves the permission to proclaim their own personal opinions

on which they confer that authority which they more or less covertly question him who by divine right possesses such a protected and awesome charism. And they even consent that each one in the Church may think and believe what he wants....

"[*Humanae vitae*] is, ultimately, a defense of life, the gift of God, the glory of the family, the strength of the people. God grant also that the lively discussion which our encyclical has aroused may lead to a better knowledge of the will of God" (NC [Foreign] News, August 24, 1968).

When this visit was ended he had his Secretary of State, Amleto Cardinal Cicognani, tell papal representatives all over the world that, in view of the "bitterness" which *Humanae vitae* has caused, "all priests, secular and religious, and especially those with responsibility as general and provincial superiors of religious orders...to put forward to Christians this delicate point of Church doctrine, to explain it, and to vindicate the profound reasons behind it. The Pope counts on them and on their devotion to the Chair of Peter, their love for the Church, and their care for the true good of souls" (*NC News*, September 6, 1968).

As far as 51 priests in the Archdiocese of Washington were concerned the Pope could count on nothing of the kind. These priests were ready for public battle over contraception, even before the encyclical was in the offing.

The international notoriety of these 51 priests (later to be scaled down to the "Washington Nineteen"), in their contest with Patrick Cardinal O'Boyle had its beginning in Baltimore, not Washington. Lawrence Cardinal Shehan of Baltimore saw a need in 1967 of *Guidelines for the Teaching of Religion*. Because part of the Washington archdiocese overlapped the State of Maryland, he persuaded Cardinal O'Boyle to make the project a common enterprise. Such collaboration made sense. The early draft of these *Guidelines* caught the attention of diocesan education officers in faraway places, because two years after the Council's close strange things were going on in the religion classrooms of the nation. On the advice of some priests a section was added to the *Guidelines* on contraception which instructed the teacher that "he may not permit or condone contraceptive practices." A year later when the *Guidelines* were to be ratified by the two Cardinals for use in both dioceses (Catholic Standard [Washington] June 27, 1968), the *Washington Archdiocesan Council of High School Teachers* called the guidelines "triumphal as well as negative in content," objectionable too because they were drafted without prior consultation with the Council. Though no one knew at the time, *Humanae vitae* was only four weeks away.

At this moment Father John E. Corrigan, Chairman of the executive committee of the *Association of Washington Priests* intervened. The Association, which began as a Vatican II Study Club, followed the pattern set by Msgr. John Egan of Chicago, who developed there a priest's association distinct from the Priest's Senate. (The Senate is the only organization recommended by Vatican II.) Priests' associations because they are voluntary, usually represent only a minority of priests, whereas the Priest's Senate collaborates with the bishop of each diocese representing the interests of all priests. The *Washington Association* sounded the second protest against the *Guidelines* releasing a "statement of conscience" for 142 of the 1,200 priests in Washington, D.C. Calling some magisterial and doctrinal tenets "mere theological tenets," Corrigan stated that "the bishops issuing the guidelines in and of themselves do not constitute the authentic magisterium." Because Corrigan's group favored the approach of the *Dutch Catechism*, the *Guidelines* of Cardinals Shehan and O'Boyle were accused of adding to confusion in the Church.

On July 29, 1968 (as if anticipating the momentary release of the Pope's long awaited decision—the press had advance copies) Charles Curran was quoted in the *Washington Star*:

> "I believe the majority of contemporary theologians and Catholics today believe Catholic

couples are free in conscience to use contraception in the responsible exercise of their marital relationship. I believe the bishops as well as all the people of the Church should speak out to prevent the Pope from making a statement that would merely reaffirm the former teaching of the hierarchical magisterium…. It seems incredible that the Pope should be thinking of such a statement…. It would be disastrous."

Diocesan Corrigan had arranged a press conference for July 30, 1968, in the Mayflower Hotel to protest the *Guidelines*. Curran took over that room for his own protest against *Humanae vitae*, leading some to conclude that Corrigan, who participated in Curran's July 28th meeting was an active participator in Curran's well-planned strategy to mount an all out campaign against any encyclical forthcoming from Rome. In return, Corrigan received support from Curran's group in his confrontation with Cardinal O'Boyle. (Without the tactical assistance of professors at the *Catholic University of America*, the celebrated "War on the Potomac" might have failed quickly.)

On July 31, 1968, the American bishops called upon "priests and people to receive with sincerity what he [the Pope] has taught, to study it carefully and to form their consciences in its light" (*NC News*).

On August 1, 1968, Cardinal O'Boyle told his priests that they must follow *Humanae vitae*. He issued a pastoral letter (August 2, 1968) which said in part:

"The Church can do without the dissent of those gentlemen who forget that in the Catholic Church even the most expert theologian must accept the teaching authority of the Church—that authority which resides in the bishops, and especially in the successor of Peter. Pope Paul listened to the theologians and to the rest of the Church, in fact to the whole world—for five long years, now it is our turn to listen to him."

For the 51 dissenters the conscience was the independent judge of moral doctrine and the opinion of dissenting theologians and alternative to the Church's authentic teaching.

On August 4, 1968, Father T. Joseph O'Donoghue— the priest who after his defection headed up the short-lived *National Council of the Laity* was suspended. The confrontation was on.

O'Donoghue later told a rally which included Protestants:

> "You are saying what our brethren of other faiths have long been waiting for you to say, something we have not clearly said since the Reformation. Namely, that Catholics are men and women of faith who in conscience listen to the word and in conscience decide" (*Washington Post*, September 16, 1968).

On August 10, 1968 Cardinal O'Boyle wrote to each of the dissenters a ten-page letter explaining the historical background of the problem and the present status of doctrine and dissent, concluding with the following official policy for his priests:

> "Since I am the Bishop of Washington, you recognize me as a successor of the apostles sent by Christ. I have commissioned you to teach and preach Catholic doctrine, and to exercise your pastoral ministry both in confession and out of it in strict accordance with the authentic teaching of the Catholic Church. To present this teaching merely as one alternative is not in accordance with it. I cannot allow you to diverge from this teaching, because I can only authorize you to do what I am authorized to do myself."

Not only was this a customary statement from a Catholic bishop, but a standard response from a chief executive of any enterprise which expects discipline among officials.

The *New York Times* editorialized (October 1, 1968) that O'Boyle's mistake was refusing to accept dissent, in view of the Catholic trend to use contraceptives anyway.

The *Washington Evening Star* lamented (October 3, 1968) the "tragic escalation" as a result of O'Boyle's stand: "Despite Pope Paul's refusal to move the Church off its present stand on birth control, such a move will come soon. No organization, spiritual or temporal, can long disregard the overwhelming sentiments of its members.

Some Catholic statements were more unsympathetic. John B. Mannion, former executive secretary of the *Liturgical Conference*, thought Cardinal O'Boyle had "blown his cool." Defending the dissenters, Mannion said their most deeply felt fear was "the prospect of not being a priest." (At least 25 of the 51 ultimately left the priesthood.) Mannion concluded:

> "We see at work in the birth control issue the celibacy debate, the germinal drive for divorce and remarriage, the frequency of intercommunion, and [in] a number of more doctrines such as purgatory, hell, transubstantiation, Mary as co-redemptrix, and so on. What a decade it is going to be for the O'Boyle's of this world."

In his delineation of the issues Mannion was perfectly correct. (*Commonweal*, October 18, 1968).

On the other side of the dispute few people at the time took notice that two days after *Humanae vitae* (August 1, 1968) the *Washington Star* polled 315 priests to discover that 203 supported the Pope. Notice had been given to the 13 Jesuits at Georgetown University who opposed O'Boyle, but not much attention to the 17 Jesuits there who supported him. No significance at all was seen in Catholic University's Father Robert L. Faricy's immediate withdrawal from dissent when it was clear that Curran and company were turning the difference into an authority fight. Less public comment was made later when Jesuit Faricy's contract at Catholic University was not renewed. During the weeks following the publication of *Humanae vitae* O'Boyle was a busy man. Forced to discipline a minority of his diocesan priests he found more testy opponents among the priests at the *Catholic Uni-*

versity of America, of which he was Chancellor. (In any Pontifical Catholic University established under a Papal Charter the Chancellor is the man assigned by the Holy See as the guarantor of orthodoxy.) After listening to what CUA dissenters had to say, O'Boyle was prompted to make a poignant observation: "I wonder whether theology is not being perverted from its high office in the service of the Catholic faith into an instrument for destroying the faith we have received and replacing it with a new set of man-made ideas" (*NC News*, August 22, 1968).

O'Boyle, of course, was not without resources—and supports of his own. A flight to Rome on August 10, 1968, brought assurance from Pope Paul VI that the Pope intended *Humanae vitae* to be taken as a full affirmation of the Catholic teaching. Returning to his see, the Cardinal insisted (August 31, 1968) that dissenters accept the authentic teaching of the Church, especially in their classroom activity, confessional practice, and counselling, at the same terminating public dissent. The dissenting priests' answer was continued insistence on the superiority of conscience. When he announced his decision in the pulpit of St. Matthew's Cathedral, the mass-attenders cheered. All during this protracted dispute his personal mail ran heavily in his favor.

For enforcing the encyclical at a time when the entire American culture was going through its worst anti-authority days, the Cardinal of Washington paid a price. He was picketed at the Shrine of the Sacred Heart on the occasion of the Labor Day Mass, September 2, 1968. The following day at the Cathedral Latin School he was greeted with obvious hostility by the media representatives. That night on national television the edited version of the press conference made the hearty and friendly Cardinal look unbending and grimacing.

On October 9, 1968, Cardinal O'Boyle instructed his priests further:

> "I do not accept an opinion concerning conscience that reduces the Church of Christ to the role of just one more advisor among many."

This was and still is the key issue in the dispute.

The contest with his priests continued for two years, until September 1, 1970. Thirty-eight priests still remained under discipline. During this period Cardinal O'Boyle expended from diocesan monies more than $100,000 toward the maintenance of these priests—over and above what they received from their pastors or former pastors.

Pope Paul VI encouraged Cardinal O'Boyle (May 15, 1969) with this assurance: "Not only did you give immediate acceptance of the teaching of the magisterium, but you also strove, with exemplary and apostolic concern, that all priests and laity should give the same acceptance." By this time O'Boyle had initiated scores of interviews, individually and in groups, with the priests who were giving him trouble. With encouragement from the Pope, the Archbishop of Washington returned to these men (June 27, 1969), on the first anniversary of *Humanae vitae* seeking agreement with the following statement:

> "Having considered the message addressed to us by the Holy Father, I respond by declaring that I accept the teaching of *Humanae vitae* as the authentic teaching of the Church with regard to contraception and shall follow it without reservation in my teaching, preaching, counselling and hearing confessions."

A few of the dissenting priests accepted O'Boyle's offer at this juncture. Father Corrigan celebrated the anniversary of *Humanae vitae* (August 3, 1968) with an irregular liturgical ceremony in a Protestant church.

The "Washington Nineteen" took their case to Rome in 1970, although by this time no one knew for sure the exact number of priests still under discipline. On April 26, 1971, the *Congregation for the Clergy* issued the verdict which prompted the *New York Times* (April 30, 1971) headline: *Vatican Rules Against Priests Who Disagreed on an Encyclical.* Not only did the Vatican find that Cardinal O'Boyle followed canonical procedures, but that his theology was also soundly Catholic. The document read:

"The ordinary magisterium, i.e., the Pope and the Bishops in their local churches, has the duty and responsibility to teach on matters pertaining to faith and morals....

"Those who receive canonical faculties of a diocese are assumed to communicate this teaching, according to the traditional norms of the Church, to those under their care."

However, the priests who were still functioning were not required to withdraw their public rejection of *Humanae vitae*.

Ten years earlier priests would not publicly contest their bishop on a matter of doctrine, agitate the Catholic faithful or divide their loyalties. The ongoing dialogue over three years did not seem to solve anything, since the confrontation was politically motivated.

Cardinal O'Boyle stood up for the Catholic principle of Church organization and was vindicated in the end. But he did seem to stand alone.

11. What About the Other Bishops?

The pastoral problems—after as well as before the encyclical—were many. The bishops as a body may not have been as permissive as they appeared because the dissident priests were comparatively few and these few in most cases issued only one press release and were heard from no more in public. Had CUA clubs existed in other dioceses with the same determination to establish ongoing dissidence against local bishops as the Curran-Corrigan group did, there probably would have been more suspended priests.

Even without Washington-type confrontations, bishops were required to deal with pastoral confusion. During the length of the controversy, contraceptives had been blessed in some confessionals, but not in others. The use of contraceptives by married couples was a grave matter and serious sin, if all other conditions for serious sin were present. What would Church authority do about dissent in the bedroom? Historically, the Church has been strict with its people only when the people themselves were disciplined in the practices of Catholic life. Stricter in the early Church than later, in Ireland and Poland more than France or Italy, in small towns more than in cities, whatever the reason, the "power of loosing" rather than the "power of binding" was to be a matter of silent policy during the post *Humanae vitae* turbulence. Some looked upon this as retreat from the high standards of observance to which the American Church had become accustomed. In a sense it was. But most American priests, even after *Casti connubii* (1930), preached a firm Gospel in the pulpit, while practicing mercy in the confessional. Absolution was rarely denied to Catholics practicing "birth control," unless arrogance or defiance appeared in the penitent. Customarily, the promise "to try" to cure contraceptive habits, as would be sought for other sexual sins, was sufficient to gain penitents' absolution.

The difference in recent pastoral practice is the new phenomenon of priests sanctioning contraception and sexual sins of all kinds. The new approach is alleged to be a reaction to the puritanical attitudes of the 19th century Church. Factually, however, sexual sins were always major objects of the Church's penitential discipline precisely because their privacy and their power made self-control by the individual or social control by the Church (or society) rather difficult. The Church intervened in these matters where few others dared—in the consciences of her faithful.

The pastoral problem now—after as before the encyclical—would be to raise the sights of Catholic people so that they understood where virtue lay, to move (even prod) them to make themselves virtuous as the Church understood that term.

It is in this area of the formation of conscience that Church authorities recently have created some of their own problems. Rome prompted national hierarchies to respond to the encyclical and they did, most of them reaffirming the papal ban without equivocation. The Holy See apparently did not expect that some hierarchies might blur the teaching. Pastoral practice (binding or loosing) always varies from nation to nation. African bishops had no problem with *Humanae vitae* because Africans—an unsophisticated people—were not contraceptionists. Nor did the Philippine bishops. These statements were ignored by the American press because they were strict *(NC News,* November 7, 1968). The Australian bishops told their people: "Every member of the Church must be considered bound to accept the decision given by the Pope. To refuse to do so would be a grave act of disobedience" *(NC News,* August 10, 1968). (The Australian bishops recently felt compelled to restate that the Church ban on contraception binds all "without ambiguity" *(Tablet,* Brooklyn, February 17, 1977). The Mexican bishops: "It is never licit to accept the opinions of theologians against the constant teaching of the Church" *(NC News,* August 13, 1968). The Bishops of England and Wales took note of conscience but stressed the necessity of a conscience formed by doctrine *(NC News,* October 4, 1968).

The secular press and the dissenting theologians, however, were not interested in affirmation and reaffirmation. They wanted confirmation of the right to have two contrary doctrinal positions and still be "loyally Catholic." Here the French, Dutch, Canadian, German, Austrian and Scandinavian hierarchies provided statements which gave the press the seeming loopholes they sought. They have been exploiting these loopholes ever since.

The Dutch statements were the most damaging chiefly because the secular press had come to realize how newsworthy Holland's hierarchy was from the moment in March, 1963 when Bishop W. Bekkers made it clear on television that people must make up their own minds on contraception *(Herder Correspondence,* October, 1963). *Humanae vitae* was no sooner made public than the Dutch hierarchy was being cited as leaving the matter to conscience, regardless of what the Pope said. The first Sunday after publication (August 4th) sermons throughout Holland told churchgoers that the final decision must be made by them (NC [Foreign] News, August 9, 1968). Msgr. H. J. Roygers, Vicar General of the Breda diocese, declared: "A papal encyclical has no other authority than the force of the arguments used. The Pope is not infallible, only the Church is infallible, i.e., the Pope together with his bishops and priests" (NC Foreign News, July 30, 1968). The American-born Bishop of Stockholm, John E. Taylor, O.M.I., pointed out that the encyclical "does not have to be regarded as infallible" and "no one should act against the conscience" (NC Foreign News, August 5, 1968). The French bishops took a different tack but ended up going in the same direction. Conceding that "contraception can never be a good," they leave the decision with couples, if they face a conflict of duties between their service to each other and to Church teaching.

Closer to home the Canadian bishops made a statement which some now regret. But in 1968 these bishops, while asserting solidarity with the Pope, refrained from endorsing his reaffirmation of the immorality of contraception. They did not encourage dissenters but consoled the faithful, talked about a conflict of duties. Their remarks were interpreted by Canadian reporter Douglas J. Roche as (1) upholding the prohibition of contraception as an ideal; (2) permitting those in good conscience to receive Holy Communion without going to confession first (Commonweal, October 18, 1968). Bishop Alexander Carter, president of the Canadian Catholic Conference, was quoted (Washington Post, September 25, 1968) as saying:

> "We know there are going to be days and times when they are not going to know how to live up to this ideal.... If the time comes for them to make a decision on contraception and if they are convinced they are doing their best, they should not feel they are violating God's word."

The American bishops, on the other hand, were more consistent in their response to Paul VI but found difficulty anyway. Part of their problem originated with their soft first response which merely asked people "to receive it (the encyclical) with sincerity, to study it carefully and to form consciences in its light." Several dissenting theologians leaped on that sentence to argue this is what they had been saying. Bishop Joseph Bernardin, then general secretary of the National Conference of Bishops, immediately denied this, insisting (what dissenting theologians do not insist) that the consciences were to be formed correctly.

Their collective pastoral *Human Life in Our Day* (November 15, 1968) repeated standard Catholic theology.

1. Contraception is objectively evil.
2. Circumstances reduce guilt.
3. Sinners should use the sacrament of Penance and the Eucharist.
4. Disagreeing theologians have to follow the Church's rules on such matters.

However, because words like "conscience," "reduced moral guilt," "licit theological dissent," all technical theological concepts, appeared in a statement intended to be read in lay language, the media were able to distort the tenor of its content. One New York radio station on Friday night said, "The American bishops have approved a limited use of contraceptives for Catholic couples." The *New York Times* headlined the story for Saturday (November 16th): *Bishops Temper Curbs on Birth Control. The Washington Eveningstar* on the same day had this lead-in: *Bishops Back Birth Edict. Note Roles of Conscience: Prelates Assert Church Shouldn't Deny Sacraments.* The *New York Times* on Sunday in its "Review of the Week" reported that no matter what the thrust of the pastoral, a "loophole" had been provided for a Catholic to practice contraception.

Loopholes were sought or invented. Father John B. Sheerin, C.S.P., in a foreword to the Paulist Press edition of the Pastoral himself invented a loophole which is not in the text. Quoting the bishops who asked those "who have resorted to artificial contraception never to lose heart but to continue to take advantage of the strength which comes from the Sacrament of Penance," then (p. 7) Sheerin added his own obiter dicta "without saying they must go to confession." The bishops could not mean this because the Sacrament of Penance involves confession. Unquestionably, some priests and couples found the same loophole—the bishops not seeming to anticipate how the sentence would be interpreted. Sheerin also raises in his foreword (p. 11) what he calls "unanswered questions" about the encyclical: Why was it not the decision of the Council rather than the Pope alone? Why did the Pope keep the matter off the Bishops 1967 Synod agenda in Rome? Will papal authority be irretrievably damaged by dissent? Questions raised about the encyclical in a publication of the bishops' own pastoral did not help the literal credence of the pastoral itself.

On the other hand, Kenneth Woodward, religious editor of *Newsweek*, an active proponent of contraception himself saw the exact meaning of what the American bishops had said. *Newsweek* (November 25, 1968) reported: "Unlike the liberal Dutch and French bishops, the Americans showed scant respect for the supremacy of conscience—particularly in the face of debatable teaching. They were chiefly concerned with defending the teaching authority of the Church."

This review of bishops' reactions to *Humanae vitae* prompts the question first raised by St. Paul in the early Church: "If the bugle call is uncertain, who will get ready for battle?" (1 Cor. 14:18) Pope Paul's bugle call is clear enough. But some generals in the field sounded a different tune. Bishop John Wright of Pittsburgh placed a finger on the problem *(NC News*, August 2, 1968) when, after denying that the Pope had consigned to Gehenna Catholics trapped in contraception, gave stern warning to those who foster, counsel, or impose what is wrong, especially if they are spiritual directors. Father John C.

Ford, S.J., also took *America* magazine to task for seeming to suggest that Cardinal O'Boyle restore his dissenting priests in a spirit of reconciliation (April 25, 1970), accusing O'Boyle of being unfair, inequitable, and unjust.

Father Ford made two important rejoinders to this editorial (May 30, 1970):

> 1. "No group of priests has the right of public, scandalous dissidence from their own bishop on a point of doctrine that he is teaching with the explicit support of the Holy Father."
> 2. "When priests publicly and persistently refuse to do so, their bishop is bound in conscience to withdraw their authorization."

Editor Donald Campion's, S.J., view of reconciliation was rejected by the Holy See in 1971, but his reply to Father Ford in 1970 rejected the Ford reading. He denies Ford's "talent for interpreting papal letters that is not granted to the hierarchies of several nations" *(America,* May 30, 1970).

Pope Paul VI never expressed a word of approval for the hierarchical statements of Holland, France, Sweden, or Canada, as he praised Cardinal O'Boyle's stand on *Humanae Vitae* many times, but as long as bishops themselves were counted as dissidents, and remained unreproved, the suspicion circulated that Rome might settle this problem fraudulently by holding to its anti-contraceptive terminology, while countenancing "exceptions." This would make the encyclical in time a dead letter. Some scholars say this now.

12. The Alleged Right To Dissent

Probably there is no more serious question to be faced by the officers of the Catholic Church than the alleged right to dissent claimed by contemporary theologians. It makes no difference what the Church says about anything if theologians—eminent or pedestrian—can set themselves up as rival teachers of the Gospel. It makes little difference whether the questioned teaching is infallible, because dissenters, who once resisted non-infallible statements (the Mosaic authorship of the Pentateuch, religious freedom in civil society, the primary and secondary purposes of marriage), now argue over admittedly infallible positions of the Church (on Christ's nature, Mary's role in redemption, the primacy and infallibility of the Pope).

Other Christian Churches do not have this difficulty. They define themselves differently, usually as congregations or assemblies of believing Christians with a common fellowship in their faith, who celebrate this faith through common prayer, and share a common understanding of what Christ wants. But evangelical churches never claim to *stand as mediators between* Christ and the believer.

The Catholic Church makes this claim. The Catholic Church claims to speak with the authority Christ gave, asserts its right to bind and loose, not only conduct but minds. The assumption of Catholic faith is that the believer is willing to make that submission. If he does not, he cannot remain a Catholic, at least not for long.

Therefore, in the Catholic Church two voices of Christ, if it means the Church formally teaches two different things as Christ's mind, cannot co-exist. Two voices saying that Christ did, did not rise from the dead; Mary is, is not a virgin; the Church is, is not divinely established; bishops are, are not, the successors of the apostles, cannot be simultaneously true. A great deal of speculation can go into explaining how these "mysteries" of Catholic faith are true, but not that they might be false. That is speculation reserved for unbelievers. Dissent as defined by contemporary theologians means two rival teaching voices in theory, and two different churches in practice.

The fact that the Jewish and Protestant religious traditions provide living space within the same body for contradictory Orthodox, Conservative, Reform styles of believing and behaving is not reason for the Catholic Church to consider these acceptable models. Factually, the genius of the Church is its ability to tolerate high, middle, and low behavior patterns in her people, *while insisting on one creed, one code, one cult.* Decisions about Catholic truth are made authoritatively, not as the result of consensus among theologians. *Church authority permits theologians, as special experts in God's word, to counsel the faithful authoritatively.* When the Church clearly states doctrine it denies permission—explicitly or equivalently—to anyone to teach or preach other than what was authentically pronounced as coming from Christ. The modern dissenting theologian denies the Church this authority, placing himself between pastors of souls and the faithful as an alternate voice of Christ, considering it his right and duty over the heads of those pastors to oppose what they authentically teach.

In two millennia ground rules have developed for expressing theological opinions, which permitted development while preventing wild speculation or irresponsible behavior from weakening the faith of Catholic people or compromising high Church standards. Five basic rules have come to govern theological speculation which contravened existing Catholic formulas.

1. Believing Catholics may not openly dissent from their faith.

2. Pastors of souls may not accept dissenting views as norms of parochial ministry.

3. The faithful may not follow the opinions of dissenting theologians in practice.

4. Theologians may research Church questions freely but if they doubt the validity of any teaching they must bring their doubts and evidence discreetly and privately to the attention of Church authority.

5. Catholics in doubt about a noninfallible teaching may suspend or withhold their assent, while they take every opportunity to resolve their difficulty through study, consultation or prayer.

The mature understanding of theologians who developed these principles are many. A few typical citations reveal the flavor of their thinking.

D. Palmieri (Tractatus De Romano *Pontifice* 1931, p. 551).

"[The Pope] must not be publicly contradicted, nor may an opposing doctrine be publicly defended, unless that he himself permits the matter to be debated by Catholics so that truth more clearly be revealed or to provide a period of study leading to solemn definition, or for some other reason."

J. M. Herve (Manuale Theologicae Dogmaticae Volume I, 1935, pp. 551ff.

"Noninfallible doctrinal pronouncements from the Pope or from the Roman Congregation are universally obligatory—[this] does not prevent anyone from raising questions and respectfully proposing to legitimate authority arguments—[then] it is permissible for him to suspend internal assent—[but] he must maintain external respect for the decree as long as it remains in force."

G. Van Noort (Dogmatic Theology, 1961, p. 275) calls *magisterium* "a practically certain expert" so that when assent may legitimately be suspended, the posture is still one of reverence."

The only author, cited by Charles Curran *(Dissent in and for the Church,* p. 12) who can be said to offer him a handle for his own dissidence is Otto Karrer *(Handbuch Theologischer Grundegriffe,* Volume 2, 1967, p. 274) which reads:

"These personal (i.e. of the Pope) and curial pronouncements demand reverential assent *salva conscientia,* that is with the right of conscience respected."

In summary, dissidence within the Church came to be exercised according to these norms.

—Noninfallible teaching required assent from all Catholics.

—Outward disobedience is always excluded.

—Noninfallible teaching can be refined by further study

—The presumption of truth is on the side of magisterium.
—Magisterial officers are in control of the findings from research.

Traditional doctrine did not really sanction dissent at all. It permitted withholding assent during private research. A rival teaching office to magisterium by the nature of things was excluded. This policy resulted in the adoption of Canon 2317 of the *Code of Canon Law* (1918), which, referring specifically to noninfallible teachings, reads:

> "All who obstinately teach or either publicly or in private defend a doctrine that has been condemned by the Apostolic See or by an ecumenical council, but not as a formal heresy, are to be excluded from the ministry of preaching the Word of God or hearing confessions, and from any office of teaching. This in addition to the penalties which the sentence of condemnation decrees against them and the penalty which the Ordinary, after a due warning, may consider necessary to repair the scandal given."

After the Council's close, the First Synod of Bishops took up the relationship of theologians to the authentic magisterium, and while bishops were encouraged to seek the advice of theologians and encourage their investigations, they—the bishops—were to protect the magisterium by repeated proclamation of its content (*NC News*, September 5, 1968). This position favors the rights of Church authority. The burden of proof always remained on change-makers. Bishops and Rome did not invoke traditional sanctions against dissenters. But neither did they accept the rationale justifying dissent.

A variety of arguments has been assembled to bolster the case against what was called an uncreative hierarchy. One argument alleges that (1) bishops and Pope have erred in the past because theologians were not consulted and (2) another that doctrinal development is due to inventive theologians working outside teaching formulas. However, the function of the Catholic theologians to propose new propositions does not imply that their function to invent incorporates the right to determine the orthodoxy of the inventions.

The more fundamental and substantial arguments for dissent can be summarized under four headings.

First, the effort of dissenters to reinterpret the decrees of the Second Vatican Council.

Secondly, the effort to redefine Catholic theology.

Thirdly, the effort to create a second magisterium in the Church.

Fourthly, the effort to redefine the Catholic Church.

While many theologians can be cited to defend one or all of these arguments, this presentation will confine itself to the writings of moralists Charles Curran and Richard McCormick.

1. Reinterpretation of Vatican II

Charles Curran and his co-authors in *Dissent In and For the Church* (pp. 100-101) speak as follows:

> "With all reverence, theologians recognize that the documents of Vatican II were 'dated' on the first day after solemn promulgation....
>
> "The spirit of Vatican II might be ignored in favor of the letter and limitations of officially promulgated formulations. Reference in the future to the letter of the pronouncements of Vatican II as the final norm for evaluating data would bring Roman Catholic ecclesiological progress to a halt. This is not because Vatican II formulations are unsuitable; rather, it is because they are intrinsically limited to what the Council Fathers intended them to be—formulations which express, for the most part, the maximum capacity of that time but which do not preclude future, ongoing developments beyond the categories of Vatican II itself."

If that statement was made in 1998, thirty-three years after Vatican II, when the Church had evaluated the practical effect of 1965 decrees, the pluses and minuses, and the new needs of the Church seen by magisterium, the previous paragraphs might be reasonable statements for reforming an aging status quo. But these lines were penned in 1965 before the Pope's signature on documents was hardly written, before anyone knew what Vatican II meant, before the Holy See itself had organized implementing decrees!

The practical import of the Curran thesis is that documents—any documents, including the most sacred —have no real binding power in what they say. For dissenters, they are at best useful tools for subjectively interpreting what they really mean. If, for example, the Council rejected, as it did, the move of *periti* to separate the *unitive* from the *procreative* purposes of marriage, or the *collegiality* of bishops from the *primatial* power of the Pope, then argues Curran, those restrictive documents must not be allowed to inhibit immediate moves to complete the job he thinks should have been done. Within this ideology it is impossible to have dissent because it is impossible to have orthodoxy.

2. Redefinition of Catholic Theology

Process theology is an invitation to religious skepticism. As the argument is developed: Revelation comes from study, not from God; it is a process, never an offer of final truth; statements by the Church as to what revelation is, says, teaches, requires, must always be subject to personal reinterpretation; if at any given time statements of the Church are taken simply as truth itself, without scrutiny, reexamination or retesting "new truths" will never be discovered and the Church stands still. Presumably, the best interpreters of Church statements are theologians, the suppliers of "new truths."

There is enough plausibility in this position to gain it a superficial hearing. Development of doctrine comes because the Church gains new insights into unchangeable truths when it applies the Gospel principles to situations which are different from one century to the next. The challenge of atomic war or genetic engineering were not the things Peter and Paul faced. However, there are also constants in Christianity—Jesus is God, Mary is a Virgin, there is a heaven, adultery (even contraception) is wrong. All the ratiocination does not alter the basic reality of their simple meaning given by Christ Himself.

Even the simple truth that the *magisterium* decides when "the process" comes to a halt, when the presumed man of faith accepts or does not accept (assents or dissents to) the "truth" of faith, when "the faithful" are called to say Credo is a *constant*. The reason why so many theologians did not like Pope Paul's "Credo of the People of God" is because it laid stress on the constants cf Christianity.

A theology which is "in process" indefinitely is not Catholic theology. A theology which no longer finds certitude in what the Church defines as absolutely certain is not Catholic theology. A theology which does not recognize that it is at the service of magisterium, not magisterium itself, is not Catholic theology.

Once Charles Curran led his 87 dissenters in public revolt against *Humanae vitae*, the *Committee on Doctrine for the Catholic Bishops* was forced to say that contemporary theologians were insensitive to the pastoral care of the faithful and minimized the importance of magisterium. To correct and alleviate the scandal caused, Bishop Bernardin arranged a meeting in the Statler Hotel, New York City, August 18-19, 1968 between four American bishops, six dissenters, and four auditors. These included Bishops Joseph Bernardin, Philip Hannon, John Wright and Alexander Zaleski; dissenters Charles Curran, John F. Hunt, Daniel Maguire, Walter Burghardt, Bernard Häring, James McGivern, acting rector of Catholic University John P. Whelan; and three nondissenters: Carl Peter, Paul McKeever, and Austin Vaughan. Bernardin at the outset had hopes the dissenters would move toward a position more acceptable to the bishops. But that never materialized. Some of the dissenters admitted they wanted to create a crisis. Besides elevating their own role in the Church, they reduced the Pope's role radically. Some even wanted the bishops to disagree with the Pope. The capstone of the entire meeting was the threat by one scientific theologian that, if the bishops used penalties against them, as many as 20,000, including nuns, would leave the Church!

3. A New Status for Theologians

The claim that there is a second magisterium in the Church—staffed by theologians—has brought this response from Jesuit Joseph F. Costanzo, who, while at Fordham University evaluated this claim:

"The insistence [of dissenters] that theologians are intrinsic to the ecclesial magisterium is the most rootless of all protestations. There is no warrant for it in the mandate of Christ, neither explicitly, implicitly, or by any manner of prolonged inferential ratiocination. There is no evidence of such a role for theologians in the writings of the Fathers of the Church nor in any of the official documents of the Church, papal or conciliar. And for all the dissidents' facile rhetorical references to Vatican II, the Council Fathers never graced them with a distinct classification or separate consideration as they did with the Roman Pontiff, the bishops, the religious, laity and priests. Indeed, the word itself "theologians" appears *only once* among the 103,014 words of the sixteen official texts promulgated by the Ecumenical Council. Considering the centrality of the dissidents' concept of the role of theologians as 'an intrinsic element in the total magisterial function of the Church' to their ecclesiology, it seems that they have been slighted by a Council celebrated for its formulation of the collegiality of bishops and by those very bishops who were accompanied by *periti*" (*Thomist*, October, 1970).

4. The Redefinition of the Catholic Church

Richard McCormick rightly concludes that concepts about the binding force of Church teaching and the right to dissent are closely tied into what one thinks about the Catholic Church. He writes:

> "If a heavily juridical notion of the Church prevails, is it not inevitable that a heavily juridical notion of the magisterium will accompany this? This means that the teaching office of the Church could easily be confused, to some extent or other, with the administrative (or disciplinary) office....
>
> "The Second Vatican Council enlarged our notion of the Church by moving away somewhat from the juridical model. The dominant description of the Church became the People of God. If this notion of the Church is weighed carefully, would it not affect the notion of the Church as teacher? Just one of the effects would be a clearer separation of teaching and administration (discipline). In the light of this separation magisterial teachings would not be viewed as 'imposed,' commanded, demanding submission, and obedience, for these terms suggest disciplinary jurisdiction, not teaching authority. Rather, noninfallible Church teachings would be seen as offered to the faithful. Obviously, such teaching must still be viewed as authoritative, but the term 'authoritative' would shed many of its juridical, and sometimes almost military connotations. The proportionate response to authoritative teaching might not *immediately* be religious assent, even though such acceptance would generally follow" *(Theological Studies,* December, 1968, pp. 714-715).

Apart from the fact that general acceptance of Church teaching does not seem to follow after dissenting teachers have done their work, these two paragraphs lay the groundwork for McCormick's own reversal on contraception and for other theologians' dissent on more fundamental Catholic issues. Their underlying assumptions call for some scrutiny.

First, the dominant description of the Church in Vatican II is not "the People of God." That concept is merely one of seven used. It is an additional emphasis provided, but not an entirely new one. The "People of God" described in *Lumen gentium* are not a mass of flattened bodies and souls scattered across the plains of the Church, but a community of believers varying in their faith-needs, faith-responses, faith-roles, all shepherded by leaders called priests, bishops, and Pope. Priests, bishops, and Pope are very much part of the People of God and are the divinely instituted leaders of those people.

However, if dissenting scholars succeed in flattening the Church into an amorphous mass, then it is easier to make a case for a leadership other than hierarchy.

Secondly, the notion of the Church as a law-making body is central to the teaching of *Lumen gentium*. Teaching with authority is teaching within the context of discipline. A teacher with knowledge is not on the same footing as the learner. The Church does not merely give friendly advice to believers about Christ and the requirements of salvation. The classroom teacher does not place the formula two plus two equals four on that basis either. The authoritative teacher insists on his teaching—if he knows it to be true. He gives failing grades to the student who insists on writing two plus two equals five, or to the alleged believer who says Jesus Christ is not God.

If proposed as a pedagogical device for reaching unbelievers, McCormick's approach is useful. John Dewey was not the first teacher to decide that indirect discourse or the parable may be more effective tools for educating the retarded, the culturally deprived, and skeptics. But this is not the way Christ dealt with His believing disciples, nor the way the catechisms of the Church, from Augustine to Trent, taught the faithful. In these source books authoritative teachings of the Church did not merely enjoy a presumption of truth waiting for endorsement by theologians prior to intellectual commitment. The obligation of acceptance was stated unambiguously by the Church, and became incumbent on the believer, the theologian as well, to give assent. Any other principle of operation would have rendered the Church superfluous.

One thing worth noting is that although McCormick and others reject the juridical conception of magisterium, they keep a juridical or legalistic conception of obedience. They say that authority is not legalistic but then proceed to give legalistic reasons why one is at liberty to think or do as one wishes.

But a faithful person does not look at a magisterial document and ask: "Do I *have* to accept this? Or, how much of this may I deny before I run afoul of some legal-moral obligation? The faithful person instead regards the magisterium within its sphere with confidence and trust, and takes its judgments as *inherently* authoritative very much as—though for different reasons—the average person trusts a judge or a surgeon within their respective competencies.

McCormick and the other theologians do not reject this concept of authoritative competency as if they thought it had *no* application in the domain of religious truth. Rather, *they displace this sort of authority to themselves—to scholars. They do this because they think of religious truth as if it were to be gained primarily by scholarly inquiry, not as a personal truth about man's relation to God received from Him by personal communication.*

Cardinal O'Boyle met the McCormick position head on (August 21, 1968) when he confronted CUA's theologians:

> "What they are saying is either that human judgment stands above the law of God or that the Catholic Church is lying when it claims divine authority for its moral teaching" (*NC News*, September 5, 1968).

Historic Church limitations on public dissent by theologians were acknowledged by the U.S. bishops in

Human Life in Our Day (November 15, 1968). One sentence, however, written under the title "norms of licit dissent," leaves the bishops open to the charge of conceding what the Holy See might not concede: "The expression of theological dissent from the magisterium is in order only if the reasons are serious and well-founded, if the manner of the dissent does not question or impugn the teaching authority of the Church and is such as not to give scandal." It should have been clear by November 15, 1968, when this was written that the dissent going on, however serious the intent, was not well-founded in Church tradition, did impugn the teaching authority of the Church and gave scandal, if by that is meant obstacles were deliberately placed in the way of observance by the people for whom *Humanae vitae* was intended.

Why did the American bishops make the above concession?

There are those who say that the bishops were intimidated by the sheer volume of the opposing voices, amplified no doubt by sympathetic mass media. Then, the U.S. bishops were aware of what other hierarchies, notably the Canadians, had said. Some of them also believed (mistakenly) that this was a tempest which quickly would pass over so that the ship of the Church would move readily into the peaceful waters to which they were accustomed.

What is not fully documented at this time is the extent to which a few bishop-advocates of contraception kept the document from taking a stronger line. The American pastoral does support *Humanae vitae* and says nothing erroneous in doctrinal aspects of the question. But dissenters were saying and advertising widely that spouses could responsibly make birth control decisions for themselves (ignoring *Humanae vitae*, if need be). The bishops had an opportunity to condemn that opinion and did not. But withdrawing from that particular contest, they provided basis for the theologians to reaffirm their counsel to Catholic married couples.

Another unresearched aspect of the bishops' retreat was their failure to harness scholarly and popular support of the Church's position. At that point (November 15, 1968) Catholics had not been alienated as they would be later. There was also a large body of Catholic scholarship, perhaps a majority, still faithful to magisterium. Solid Catholic scholars with very few exceptions remained silent in public. The general feeling among some was that their academic reputations or careers might be hurt by vigorously confronting dissenting peers; or they felt the problem was so acute that only the hierarchy can or should handle it. In any event, the scholarly opinion which supported *Humanae vitae* was not harnassed.

13. The Aftermath of *Humanae Vitae*

In the ten years since Pope Paul VI ended the period of ambiguity and speculation about the Church's position on birth control five different trends are observable in and out of the Church:

1. The dramatic rise in the use of contraceptives by Catholics.

2. Growing concern about contraception in non-Catholic circles.

3. Grand silence about contraception by Church authorities.

4. The continuance of contradictory counsel to the Catholic faithful.

5. The rise of new support for the Papal position.

1. Catholic Contraception

Charles Westoff and Larry Bumpass, both reputable demographers, drew the contemporary Catholic picture in one short article (*Science*, January 5, 1973). Their conclusions can be summarized as follows:

1. The use of contraceptives by Catholic women increased as follows:

1955 — 30 percent
1965 — 51 percent
1970 — 68 percent
2. In 1970 the use according to age was:
20-24 — 73 percent
25-29 — 74 percent
30-34 — 68 percent
35-39 — 50 percent
3. Whereas formerly the less educated Catholics practiced birth control against Church norms, by 1970 this trend was reversed. Educated Catholic women more frequently resorted now to contraception.
4. Whereas formerly the less pious Catholics used contraception, now the committed Catholics who go to Communion at least monthly violate Catholic norms.

In 1965 only 33 percent of monthly Communion-goers, compared to 53 percent in 1970, used contraceptives. More remarkably 67 percent of this group under 30 now use contraceptives.

The Westoff-Bumpus study takes note of two trends going on among Catholics—attrition from the Church and rejection of Catholic teaching on contraception. The authors do not relate one to the other.

These data certainly lend basis to the opinion that the Catholic Church in America has lost the battle for contraception among its own faithful. The losses certainly are serious. But considering what has gone on in the Church, the remarkable data may be the percentage under 30 who *do not* use contraceptives. Andrew Greeley makes much of the argument that *Humanae vitae* caused the leakage. The situation is more complex. As the review of the years 1961-1968 has made clear, the dissenting scholars (often merely to justify their views on contraception) felt compelled to undermine confidence in the Church itself. Once people were placed into "the conscience box" for this major issue, there was only one exit permitted, if they wanted escape—rejection of the Church on many fronts, perhaps the Church itself. If one considers that the under-30 group of Catholics likely reject many doctrines—and so are nominally Catholic only —then the percent *not* using contraceptives can be called impressive. Many of them are the Catholics associated both with the pro-life and natural family planning movements.

2. Non-Catholic Contraception

Those who once were called Catholic alarmists about contraception are now being vindicated by the growing concerns about what is happening to women, children, men, and the family because of contraception. Demographer Charles F. Westoff believes that the United States is coming closer and closer to the perfect contraceptive population—i.e., a nation with no unwanted births. In one recent study he discovered only 14 percent of all births were unwanted (*Science*, January 9, 1977). As body counts go this statistic is impressive. The birth—no birth calculus, beyond demonstrating a victory for scientific sex, also has raised once more the long since sidetracked matters of human values, to say nothing of religious values, in sexual activity, natural (God-given) processes, marital stability, human health, family health, social well-being. As Americans become more technological about sex (sterilization is rapidly replacing the pill as the preferred method of child-prevention), the serious questions once raised by Catholics alone are now to the front and center of public discussion. The 1,000,000 annual abortions in the U.S. say something about American value on life. (Planned Parenthood used this figure in 1957 about the alleged "alley" abortions but this was a figure used for propaganda purposes, without basis in fact.)

Dr. Robert Kistner of the Harvard Medical School, who helped develop the pill (with Pincus and Rock), recently remarked (*Cincinnati Inquirer*, April 14, 1977): "For years I felt the pill would not lead to promiscuity. But I have changed my mind. I think it probably has—as so has the IUD."

In 1976 there were 1,000,000 teenage pregnancies.
The use of the pill, which Dr. Herbert Ratner, calls
"chemical warfare on women" is no longer the panacea it
once was thought to be. While statisticians have various
correlations between the pill and its perils—its relation to
cancer, thrombosis, gallbladder disease, erosion of cells of
the cervix, heart disease, blood vessel disease, and death
itself—it is still important in birth control procedures,
because its use is fostered by drug companies with assistance from government domestic and foreign aid agen-
cies. In 1970 the Food and Drug Administration published
a booklet called "What You Should Know About the Pill"
for distribution in every packet of oral contraceptives.
The booklet ended up not in pharmacies but in doctors'
offices, where most pill users never see it. Another FDA
warning of IUD dangers (43 deaths in recent years) also
has not found its way to the users.

Contraception has always been big American business. Profit in pills are larger than ever. Vested interests
protect those profits. Dr. Gordon Duncan, associate director of a population study center says: "There is also
very little fundamental biologic research being done that
would support innovative developments." The perfection
of a natural family method does not attract large grants
because successful research in this area has no profitable
return. More money is earned in condoms than in continence. Dr. Allan Barnes, a vice-president at the Rockefeller Foundation, adds a further indictment: "It is
entirely possible that if the ideal contraceptive were
developed today, it would never be introduced in the
United States" (New York Times, March 5, 1975). There
is not enough profit in a creative discovery of this kind.

Meanwhile another zero point has been reached—
what Kenneth Keniston of the Massachusetts Institute of
Technology calls "the emptying family." The "latchkey"
child and possibly his one other sibling grow with no care
at all, awash in skateboards and stereos, while emanci-
pated mothers work to fulfill themselves. Not only have
parents disappeared from many children's lives (two out

of five now live in a single parent family) but grand-parents, aunts, and uncles have gone as well. Since over one million children are propelled by divorce into single parent families annually the problem will get worse before it gets better.

3. The Grand Catholic Silence

Father Richard McCormick coined the expression "The Silence Since *Humanae vitae*," when he surveyed the Catholic scene on the fifth anniversary of the encyclical (*America*, July 7 and October 20, 1973). The "silence" he infers is, of course, the seeming willingness of hierarchy to let the matter of contraception in the Church rest without further confrontation. McCormick suggests that a new commission be established this time to discover what God's will on this subject really is.

Silence certainly represents a vacuum within the Church permitted to grow in Catholic catechesis on matrimony. McCormick himself claims that contraception is not necessarily evil and may occasionally be used. The magisterium, on the other hand, says contraception is always evil, a grave evil, and may never be used by a Catholic. Furthermore, a "little contraception" exists nowhere in the world. Contraception, once accepted, becomes a way of life. It logically follows, therefore, that Catholic leadership would normally follow through with counter-measures.

But articulation of the Church's position has all but disappeared from Cana and Pre-Cana Conferences, and never really became an essential part of the Marriage Encounter program. Catechetical magazines, seminars and worship for religious educators, continuing education courses for priests and religious, almost never deal with the subject. Sex education courses continue to increase in Catholic schools, aimed at training the young to become persons rather than to form them to use sexuality within a Catholic context. During 1974 the *United Nations* designated "Population Year" (initiating a series of inter-

national conferences on the subject), *Theological Studies*
(March issue) assembled an accumulated rejection of
Catholic doctrine. The Catholic archbishop of Durban,
South Africa, Denis E. Hurley, O.M.I., on behalf of the
Church, made the following contribution to the popula-
tion question:

> "To keep the Catholic conscience bound to the
> official view on birth control would, in the circum-
> stances today, require superhuman insistence on the
> part of the magisterium. This insistence is not
> manifest. Rather there is a tendency to avoid the
> topic or to treat it with tolerance or benign inter-
> pretation. So by default a major change is occurring
> in the moral teaching of the Church—which hardly
> enhances the image of the magisterium" (p.163).

Since the credibility of magisterium is clearly at
stake, the question has been raised by more than Archbishop Hurley why Catholic leadership has not been
boldly effective in helping people live Catholic married
life in conformity with the principles of *Humanae vitae*.
In small countries like New Zealand, bishops have
natural family planning centers almost in every parish
and/or town. In the United States, no nationally successful effort by the Church has yet proved its effectiveness in
forming the attitudes, supplying the knowledge and
training, or providing the support necessary to make
natural family planning work, especially among the
poor. Motivating Catholics to accept the unwanted baby
(the essential meaning of being "open" to life), which the
contraceptionist customarily destroys, has not been
dramatically noticeable in Catholic circles in recent
years.

In 1969 Cardinal O'Boyle secured an initial grant of
$800,000 from the American bishops to establish the
Human Life Foundation, which was to organize research
in natural family life procedures and educational programs. The U.S. has invested $1,500,000 in research since
then and WHO has research projects going in 20 countries. Up until 1975 no serious effort was made to bring

natural family programs into the dioceses of the country. John Kippley's *Couple to Couple League* in Cincinnati and Father Paul Marx's *Human Life Center* in Collegeville, Minnesota, were localized efforts to effectuate *Humanae vitae* principles in Catholic lives. *The Human Life Foundation of America* now promises to nationalize the effort, although it has a long way to go with only single training centers in most dioceses. The trend is changing. At the present time $4 is being invested in Foundation programs by government for every $1 contributed by the American bishops. As natural family planning takes its place with contraception as a technique of birth regulation endorsed by government, the programs of the *Human Life Foundation*, which transcend technique, continue to grow. But the Church has yet to bring *Natural Family Planning* to the parish level, where it will do the most good.

Leo Cardinal Suenen's *Love and Control* in 1964 provided an educational blueprint necessary to make Catholic principles of marital chastity work. As the *International Planned Parenthood Federation* organizes multiple fortunes and worldwide programs to influence citizens of the world toward contraception and abortion, the Catholic Church is only beginning to marshal its forces for a belated effort to back *Humanae vitae* with programs of comparable proportions and public acceptability.

4. Contradictory Catholic Counsel

Catholic priests, nuns, magazines, even diocesan newspapers, frequently do not reinforce Catholic doctrine proclaimed by bishops and Pope, which encouraged the secular press to continue its habit of reporting imminent official Catholic change. *Newsweek* (July 30, 1973, pp. 40-41), never reconciled to *Humanae vitae*, celebrated its fifth anniversary by "uncovering" an alleged statement being secretly edited for Columbian bishops which would support all forms of contraception, except sterilization and abortion. The story also placed those bishops in support of government family planning centers at which birth control pills are dispensed. A year later, the *New York Times* (January 23, 1974) published another report of a confidential Vatican circular to bishops, allegedly easing Catholic opposition to birth control.

If the secular organs continue to make repeated references to Catholic contraception, so do Church spokesmen. Parishioners have become accustomed to parish discussions where competing priests argue for and against the Pope (*Tablet*—Brooklyn, February 24, 1972). The clearest example of what the current pastoral picture is, was given by the issues of the *Brooklyn Tablet*, following a presentation made (January 9, 1975), when Msgr. Francis B. Donnelly, Brooklyn pastor and former chief judge of the diocese, wrote an article calling for Catholic obedience to the Pope's encyclical, asserting that "the teaching of theologians or of individual priests, however intelligent or persuasive, may not be preferred to the Church's official teaching." For nine months following, the readers were treated to a newspaper debate between editor, priests, subscribers and other columnists over how much attention must be paid to the Pope. Msgr. Donnelly was not lacking in supporters, but the *Tablet* editor thought the Brooklyn pastor was interfering with Vatican II guaranteed freedom of conscience and *Tablet* columnist *Mary Carson* accused Donnelly (January 9, 1975) of not understanding Church teaching on parenthood. A young Brooklyn College seminary professor nine months later (September 23, 1976) told *Tablet* readers that "in reality most Catholics don't come to a moral judgment to practice birth control by plowing through statements from magisterium.... Being good, conscientious people, they know in their heart what they must do; what Catholics who decide to practice birth control usually say is: 'I believe in my heart what I'm doing is right.'" And then the young seminary professor added, as an afterthought: "Understand here is not that birth control is right. It can never be a good."

On the other hand, in the neighboring diocese of Rockville Center, the editor of the *Long Island Catholic* provided this counsel (October 7, 1976):

> "Are we obligated then to accept the constant teaching of the Church on artificial contraception —as affirmed by the Pope and the bishops prior to *Humanae vitae*, as affirmed by the Pope in *Humanae vitae*, as affirmed by the Pope and the bishops today? Yes."

5. New Support for the Pope

The Church supported lost causes at other times in history, even when its defense of those causes was timid. A moral position, to be moral, need not have effective technological guarantees. A moral view may be correct and, if adopted, involve personal or social risk. This is evident in issues of social justice, of war and peace. The Church, for example, may state a principle on race relations without necessarily committing itself to a particular affirmative action program of government. Or may receive abuse for proposing a specific program for enforcement. Similarly, the Church can be correct on contraception without having the ability to make practical decisions of the faithful easy or palatable. Government has that same problem. Obliteration bombing can effectively terminate a war, may be the only way to win a war, and still receive condemnation on moral grounds. Gaining a good can be highly immoral if achieved wrongly. Contrariwise, a saint like St. Francis of Assisi can be holy and, by human standards, inefficient too.

Pope Paul VI waited so long to speak that in 1968 he appeared like a lonely defender of the Church's position. Ten years later, few perceived as clearly as he that sexual activity may not be separated from its procreative purpose without dire consequences for individuals, for society, and for sex and for the moral order itself. The American bishops, however, in issuing their "Catholic

Hospital Directives" in their condemnation of contraceptive or sterilizing practices in Catholic hospitals (1971) reaffirmed the necessity of these links.

Lawrence Cardinal Shehan, who in 1966 approved the majority report of the papal birth control commission, said the following five years later (*Homiletic and Pastoral Review*, November 1973):

> "The dissenters will insist it has not been proved that contraception is intrinsically evil. That may be true if one disallows the norms drawn from human nature by Paul VI, and the norms drawn from the nature and dignity of the human person as presented by Vatican II; and if one rules out the light shed by divine revelation, particularly by Paul's *Epistle to the Romans*, taken in conjunction with the constant tradition of the Church, i.e., if one approaches the problem of contraception from the purely rationalistic and not from the Christian point of view. But the whole point is that we are Christians and we have to approach the problem of contraception and family limitation and birth regulation from the Christian point of view."

Peter Riga, who was an early dissenter, changed his mind when in October 1973 he wrote for *Triumph* ("I wrote it for *Triumph*—no one else would take it."):

> "Acts which seek directly to separate sexuality from procreation have no future, and therefore are doubly sterile. They enter into no transcendent endeavor, which is precisely what the family is about. Marriage and its necessary consequence, the family, is a transcendent relationship in which two persons engage themselves and seek to perfect themselves in a common endeavor that reaches outside of the relationship, to new life, to the future of the human race, to God's glory. There is no more important or vital work than this."

Dr. Hanna Klaus, otherwise known as Sister Miriam Paul, SCMM, is a gynecologist. After seven years as a medical missioner among the Pakistani, she returned by way of Europe convinced that *Humanae vitae* was more of an ideal than a norm. Theologians whom she had met on her way home through Europe impressed her with this. Once face to face with abortion in the affluent contraceptive culture of her own country, she was forced to rethink the relationship between womanhood and contraception. Her final conclusion was that for the "feminine woman" every coitus contains within it the psychic germs of a child, that *Humanae vitae* speaks of "the integral vision of humanity beyond partial perspectives: what it proposes is not optional for human nature but completes it" *(Homiletic and Pastoral Review*, October, 1973).

The work of Doctor John Billings of Melbourne, Australia, promoter of natural family planning, is perhaps a harbinger of Pope Paul's ultimate vindication. In the 19th century the Church by taking a strong stand against craniotomy helped encourage the perfection of the Caesarian section. The hand of science, again as a result of the Church's condemnation of direct interference with life and the process of giving life, may contribute toward new developments in the science of reproduction.

14. The Ford-Grisez Thesis

Father John C. Ford, S.J., and Doctor Germain Grisez focus on the common teaching of the Church on contraception, of which *Humanae vitae* is only the latest handing on of authentic teaching. On the tenth anniversary of *Humanae vitae* in a lengthy article for *Theological Studies* (June 1978), they take up the ancient origin of the teaching, the universal scope of the teaching, and the certainty with which it has been proposed as an imperative determinant in the behavior of married Catholics.

From 1963 on, however, theologians seeking to justify contraception, after observing (correctly) that the teaching had not been formally defined, proceeded to infer (erroneously) that the doctrine had not been infallibly taught. This "dethroning" of the Church teaching enabled them (so they argued) to attack more forcibly the certainty and truth of the traditional position.

Ford-Grisez believe in the light of the way the teaching on contraception has been proposed through the centuries that the "infallibility" claim of the teaching is very much alive, that the received Catholic teaching is still being proposed infallibly by the ordinary and universal magisterium. The conditions under which the ordinary magisterium of the bishops dispersed throughout the world can proclaim the teaching of Christ infallibly have been articulated by the Second Vatican Council; Ford-Grisez argue that *Humanae vitae* meets these criteria thus making the Church doctrine a divinely guaranteed teaching.

They make an important point. Frequently, dissenters start with the assumption that teachings not formally defined are not infallible. This is not true. Many Catholic teachings are *de facto* infallibly taught, even though not formally defined. *Lumen gentium* (no. 25) reads:

> "Although the bishops individually do not enjoy the prerogative of infallibility, they nevertheless proclaim the teaching of Christ infallibly, even when they are dispersed throughout the world, provided that they remain in communion with each other and with the Successor of Peter and that in authoritatively teaching on a matter of faith and morals they agree in one judgment as that to be held definitively."

The declaration, as Council debates indicated, extends ordinary infallibility in the Church not only to matters formally revealed (e.g., divinity of Christ) but to things virtually revealed (e.g., Mary's Immaculate Conception), to what is necessarily connected with revelation (e.g., the existence of a natural moral law), to things which are to be believed *and* to things which are to be done.

The four conditions of *Lumen gentium* under which bishops, dispersed throughout the world, proclaim the doctrine of Christ infallibly, are summarized by Ford-Grisez as follows:

1. The bishops who remain in communion with one another and teach with the Pope.

2. They teach authoritatively too in a matter of faith or morals.

3. They agree on one judgment.

4. They propose this judgment as one to be held definitively.

Just as the divinity of Christ was taught by the ordinary and universal magisterium of the Church prior to its definition by the Council of Nicea in 325, so the teaching on contraception has been proposed by the Church as a teaching to be held definitively by believers. Factually, while many Arian bishops denied the doctrine of Christ's divinity before and after definition, no more than a handful of Catholic bishops during or after Vatican II denied the teaching on contraception as *the taught and believed Catholic doctrine.*

Indeed, as John Noonan abundantly documents, no Catholic theologian up until 1963 ever taught that contraception was good. What is clear also is that in spite of internal opposition, Catholic teaching was and still is proposed as the *constant doctrine of the Church.* Even when scholars—outside the Church, later within—questioned the doctrine's scriptural base or the validity of some rational arguments in its favor—the Pope and bishops continued to reaffirm the Catholic norm.

Pope Paul, while not using the term "infallible" (Pius XII did not use the term in proclaiming Mary's Assumption), does speak in solemn language. He is not speaking as another theologian, nor as one intervening in a theological dispute. The Pope is explicitly teaching a doctrine to which by divine patrimony he avers the Catholic Church is unalterably committed. He reaffirms the Church's certainty on the subject. He rejects the possibility of altering its substance.

In essence, Ford-Grisez say: If the Catholic tradition on contraception is not infallible teaching, what can be called infallible?

Even an affirmative answer to this question will not settle the argument for dissenters. But it does put the argument back in context. Michael Novak, for example, only recently has come to recognize (in the debate over the ordination of women) what he did not accept in the earlier argument over contraception:

> "For centuries the Church has had an unbroken tradition, so unchallenged that reasons for it have not been articulated. Obscurely, many persons sense some weight in those reasons" (*Commonweal*, September 2, 1977).

Christ did not win all His public debates over what He was *revealing*. The Church has also learned that the validity or certainty of a teaching does not depend for acceptance on its perusibility or on the solemnity of the preaching. Faith in the *given* teacher usually settles the argument for the believer. This does not terminate intellectual discussion because the Church, with its intellectual tradition, encourages research and investigation. Eventually formal pronouncements by the Church's teaching authority, sets parameters for theological exploration. Ford-Grisez know that scholars are tempted to read history backward and find practices, attitudes, and institutions incompatible with the law of Christ, which once were accepted or tolerated by Christians, and even by the *magisterium*, e.g., slavery. This becomes the basis of proposing contraception as a new Christian insight comparable to the Church's late acceptance of political equality. However, what the Church accepts and tolerates is quite distinct from what it teaches. Insight into the unstable mentality of modern culture enables the Church to realize why certain marriages today can be declared null and void, which formerly would not have been so understood. It does not follow, however, that the Church's teaching on the indissolubility of a sacramental marriage itself changes.

The contraception teaching must be judged in this light. An infallibly taught doctrine continues to be taught without formal definition, because factual questions keep recurring. For example, what is a contraceptive? When the Pope and the Council undertook a second study of the pill they were dealing with factual questions. If the pill could be judged noncontraceptive, at least under certain circumstances, it would not fall under the Church's general ban. The *magisterium*, never in doubt about the immorality of contraception itself, was in momentary doubt about the absolute immorality of the pill. Since *Humanae vitae* the Church is no longer uncertain even about that.

A major management problem remains, however. This is the dissonance between doctrine and practice. The issue is no longer contraception but the ability of the Church to make its doctrine live in the lives of the faithful.

CHAPTER TWO

Biblical Thoughts on "Human Sexuality"

Rev. Manuel Miguens, OFM

The subject of this discussion was suggested by a new book—*Human Sexuality*—which is "a study commissioned by the Catholic Theological Society of America" (Paulist Press: New York, 1977). The first chapter of this work (pp. 7-32) is given the title "The Bible and Human Sexuality." The following are a few reflections on the contents of this chapter, that in some way will serve as a presentation of the book itself.

In the first section of this chapter some general principles are stated (not proven) on which a correct reading of the biblical text should be grounded. These principles will be taken up in the first place. Then some particular passages of the Old Testament are taken into consideration. Significant omissions in the Old Testament are then pointed out.

General Principles

Human Sexuality contends that "The Bible should not be seen as giving absolute prescriptions with regard to sex." It is culturally conditioned, it must be seen "against the cultural and sociological conditions that characterize its era. The Bible is an historical document bearing the limitations of all historical records" (p. 9). The statement is open to criticism in several of its parts.

In the first place the Bible itself claims that in sexual matters it marks a sharp reaction to the cultural milieu of the surrounding peoples. Far from being culturally conditioned the Bible stands up against cultural conditioning in sexual matters. Chapter 18 of Leviticus is devoted to teachings concerning sexual matters but an interesting introduction leads into the subject matter: "You—the Lord says—shall not do as they do in the land of Egypt, where you once lived, nor shall you do as they do in the land of Canaan, where I am bringing you; do not conform to their customs" (v. 3). After the doctrinal instructions the author, who refers the teaching to God Himself, concludes: "Do not defile yourselves by any of these things by which the *nations* whom I am driving out of your way have defiled themselves.... You, however,...must keep *my* statutes and decrees and must *not do* any of *these abominations*...for the *men of the land who were before you* have done all these abominations...do not do any of these abominable customs" (vv. 24-30). Of course, no reference to these statements is made in the book of the Theological Society.

The principle established in these texts is the real reason why in the case of some sexual offenses an interesting remark is made. In Judges 19:30 when a woman died of brutal sexual abuse the comment of the people is this: "such a thing has not happened nor been *seen* from the day that *the children of Israel came up out of the land of Egypt* unto this day." In 2 Samuel 13:12 when Amnon was about to rape his half-sister, Tamar said: "do not force me, for no such thing *ought to be done in Israel*, you will be as one of the *base men in Israel.*" In Genesis 34:7 Jacob's sons were indignant because their sister had been raped by Shechem who "had wrought a vile deed *in Israel*...which ought not be done." In Baal Peor the Israelites did as the pagans did: "the people began to

commit (sacred) harlotry with the daughters of Moab"
(Ex. 25:1), and this is why the Lord was indignant.

The attitude of the New Testament is not different.
The author of Ephesians 4:17ff. writes to his Christians as
follows: "do not live *as the pagans* do...they have abandoned themselves to lust and every sort of lewd conduct,"
and in 5:3 it is said that "lewd conduct, promiscuity, lust
of any sort shall not be *among you*, because of your
holiness," which is a concept taken from the Old Testament: on account of their "holiness" the people of Israel
were not supposed to live as the pagans did. In Israel, as
well as in Christianity, moral standards flow from Israel's
"holiness"; and "it is I—the Lord says—that make you
holy" (Lev. 20:7f., 26).

In addition, it is not true that the Bible does not give
"absolute prescriptions with regard to sex." The statements of the Decalogue are absolute prescriptions when
they are related to God as being the only God, to His worship, to killing, stealing, respecting one's parents, etc.
One of these prescriptions is "You shall not commit
adultery" (Ex. 20:14; Deut. 5:17), and "You shall not
covet your neighbor's wife" (Deut. 5:18)—which is as absolute as all other prescriptions. The same absolute value
attaches to the prohibitions of several kinds of incest,
adultery, homosexuality, bestiality, in Leviticus 18. The
legal phrasing is the same as in other cases ("you shall not
do"). The absolute value of such prescriptions is part of
the biblical reaction to the customs of the other peoples.

In another direction, the statement that "the Bible is
an historical document bearing the limitations of all
historical records" is too broad to be absolutely true, and
in the context where it is mentioned it is wrong. The Bible is an historical document, but it also is more than that.
It is an historical document that informs us of the sexual ethics of Israel. But these sexual attitudes are not an
adjustment or conformation to the historical situations
and surrounding conditions: they are Israel's response of
faith, and implementation of God's word of revelation
that brought about a reaction to the pagan ethic customs,

and developed a moral *praxis* within Israel. First of all, the Bible is the word of God's revelation and teaching. The moral prescriptions in Leviticus 18 are the instructions that "the Lord spoke to Moses" (v. 1); they open and close with the solemn statement "I am the Lord your God" (v. 2, 30) which is also repeated in between several times (v. 4f., 6, 21). Of course, the book of the Theological Society maintains that "simply lining up a catalogue of texts does violence to biblical theology and accomplishes little of value" (v. 7). But ignoring the text of the Scriptures does even more violence to God's word, and any subjectivistic morality that ignores the biblical text is not "biblical theology" at all.

It is contended that the teaching of the Bible on these matters is historically and culturally conditioned, because "the prominence of sex in the pagan cults...constrained Israel's prophets and religious leaders to take emphatic stands on any sexual practices that seemed related to cult" (p. 8). Later on, however, Paul's moral teaching is said to have been influenced by the ethical views of the Stoics, and that is why it has to be re-interpreted. The double standard is obvious.

Human Sexuality contends, furthermore, that "the Old Testament contains a variety of theologies and attitudes regarding sexuality" (p. 7). The statement is not supported by any biblical reference. A survey of all the biblical passages dealing with sexual matters reveals a perfect uniformity in approaching this subject. As a matter of fact, most of this material is found in the legal *corpus* of the Pentateuch where the legal texts are in perfect agreement with the narratives where sexual matters are involved.

In Leviticus 18:6 a general principle of incest is formulated: "None of you shall approach to any that is near of kin to him to uncover their nakedness: I am the Lord." This agrees with the blame of Lot's daughters who lay with their father (Gn. 19:30). The law in Leviticus 18:15 states that "you shall not uncover the nakedness of (have intercourse with) your daughter-in-law, she is your son's wife." It is this principle that is operative throughout the narrative of Judah's connections with Tamar, his daughter-in-law (Gn. 38), whom he approached because he thought she was a common prostitute; but when he found out the true relationship between themselves "he had no further relations with her" (v. 26). The law in Leviticus 18:8 states that "you shall not uncover the nakedness of your father's wife: it is your father's nakedness." This is the law or rule reflected in the blame of Reuben who had relations with Billah, one of Jacob's wives (Gn. 35:22); Jacob describes such an act as a "defilement" of his bed (Gn. 49:4; 1 Chr. 5:1). One of the commandments in the Decalogue (Ex. 20:17; Dt. 5:18) is that "you shall not commit adultery," which in Leviticus 18:20 is formulated thus: "you shall not lie carnally with your neighbor's wife." Now, this is the principle operative in the episodes of Sarah, Abraham's wife, with the Pharaoh of Egypt (Gn. 12:17) and with the king of Gerar (Gn. 20:2), in the case of Rebekah with the same king (Gn. 26:10), in the incident of Joseph's temptation by Potiphar's wife (Gn. 39), and in David's affair with Bathsheba, Uriah's wife (2 Sm. 11), which also illustrates the commandment of the Decalogue's formulation in Deuteronomy 5:18: "you shall not covet your neighbor's wife."

In Leviticus 18:9 the law is that "you shall not uncover the nakedness of your sister: the daughter of your father and the daughter of your mother." It is this commandment that is at the basis of Amnon's rape of his half-sister Tamar in 2 Samuel 13, which is described as a "vile act," since "no such a thing ought to be done in Israel" (v. 12). The statement of the law is that "you shall not do the deeds of the land of Canaan" (Lv. 8:3); this is the background of the episode of Baal Peor in Numbers 25. Another law in Exodus 34:16 states that "you shall not take Canaanite wives for your sons," a law which is behind the blame expressed in the case of Isaac, Esau and Jacob (Gn. 24:3; 26:34f.; 27:46; 28:1), in the separation of marriages by Ezra (10:14-16) and Nehemiah (Neh.

13:23-29) and, after all, in the case of the punishing Flood "when the sons of God saw that the daughters of men were fair, and they took them as wives, whomsoever they chose" (Gn. 6:2). Sometimes the same law is found in different books, such as the prohibition of "bestiality" that is found in Exodus 22:28, in Leviticus 18:23 and in Deuteronomy 27:21, and of incest of various degrees that is found in Leviticus 18 and 20 as well as in Deuteronomy 27:20-23. The prohibition of adultery is found everywhere in the Old Testament. Sometimes the same penalty for the same sexual crime is established in different parts of the legal *corpus:* v. gr., "Anyone who lies with an animal shall be put to death" (Ex. 22:18); in Leviticus 20:15f. we read as follows: "if a man lie with a beast, he shall be put to death...and if a woman goes up to an animal to mate with it the woman and the animal shall be slain." The penalty for adultery appears to be the same (death) in both Leviticus 20:10 and Deuteronomy 22:22, 20f.

Obviously, a profound coherence and uniformity can be found in the several sections of the Bible dealing with sexual matters. I was not able to detect any real disagreement that could support the statement that "the Old Testament contains a variety of theologies and attitudes regarding sexuality." The authors of the book do not provide any evidence for their assertion.

Another contention of *Human Sexuality* is that "the social importance of reproduction constitutes a basic reason for early biblical teaching on sex-related matters" (p. 7). Reproduction obviously is a valid aspect to consider in any kind of teaching about human sexuality. The Bible cannot be blamed when it makes reproduction one of the basic principles on which to ground rules concerning sex-related matters. But this principle of reproduction is not stressed only by "early" biblical teaching. It is also suggested by Malachi 2:15 and, in the New Testament, by Luke 20:36: in afterlife there is no marriage "for they *cannot die* any longer," i.e., reproduction is not necessary and, therefore, marriage and the use of sex do not apply.

The "social importance of reproduction" is connected, I understand, with another statement in the same book: "Especially after the exile, the preservation and propagation of the chosen people made sexual intercourse more than simply a private affair. Sons were viewed as a gift of God (Ps. 127:3) and children as a blessing (Ps. 128:4)" (p.8). In the first place, the writings after the exile can hardly be referred to as "early" biblical teaching. Furthermore, the notion that children are a gift and a blessing of God is a basic belief of the Scriptures at all times. We can refer to the plight and prayer of unfruitful women, because they wanted this gift and blessing from God. The biblical perspective is that fruitfulness is a "blessing" and gift of God, and unfruitfulness is God's denial of a gift that he gives or does not give—beyond the sexual characteristics of the human being.

Human Sexuality mentions also taboos in the Old Testament concerning sexual matters. Among them "another taboo of the Old Testament was the exposure of the sex organs.... Nakedness...was a sign of humiliation or degradation (Gn. 9:21-23; 2 Sm. 6:20; 10:4).... The Hebrews also had horror of deformed sex organs (Dt. 23:2)." There is no question of sexual ethics in these texts. In Genesis 9:21-23 (it is the incident of Noah when he was drunk) the point is respect for one's father, even when his attitudes are undignified. In 2 Samuel 6:20 (David dances before the Ark) the point is the "dignity" of a king before his subjects. In 2 Samuel 10:4 the point (in curtailing one's clothes) is an insult to the delegation and to him who sent the delegation. In Deuteronomy 23:2 (the reference is to "crushed" or "maimed" man's organs) the point is that he is a man (not a woman!) incapable of begetting children. Another taboo is that "women are forbidden to wear men's clothes and men forbidden to wear women's clothes" (Dt. 25:5). There is no taboo there. The message is that interchange of dress between the sexes tended to result in promiscuity. Reference is also made to "the taboos against incest (Lv. 18:6-16; Dt. 27:23)." One wonders if this is just a matter

of taboos. Leviticus 18:1-5 etc. points out that the Israelites must not do *what other peoples do*. Incest was not a
taboo to others; why should it be to the Israelites? In
another direction *Human Sexuality* states that "it is to
Sirach, a true misogynist, that we owe the preservation of
the midrash on Genesis 3: 'Sin began with a woman, and
thanks to her we all must die' (Sir. 25:23); this interpretation was to become much a part of the New Testament
tradition (Rom. 5:12; 1 Cor 15:22; 1 Tm. 2:14)." Besides
the misogynism of Sirach and the description of Sirach
25:23 as a midrash, the passage of Sirach 25 does not go
beyond what we read in Genesis 3 where Eve is represented as offering the "fruit" to Adam. The same thing
applies to the passage of 1 Tm. 2:14. Beyond that, Romans 5:12 does not refer to a woman: sin and death came
through an *anthropos*, a human being (no misogynism
there); which is also the teaching of 1 Cor 15:22 when it is
realized that "Adam" is the human being.

The Understanding
of Some Basic Texts

According to *Human Sexuality*, "the Yahwist associ-
ates sexuality with the human problem of loneliness....
The first purpose of sex, as described by the Yahwist, is
mutuality, our belonging to one another.... For the
Yahwist sexuality was a gift from God, drawing people
from loneliness to relationship" (p. 8f.). The reference is,
of course, to Genesis 2:18-24 where the "rib" of Adam is
turned into a woman who is "bone of my bones" etc. The
understanding of this passage by the Catholic Theological
Society could be adduced as a solid reason for "marriages"
of two or more individuals of the same sex. After all, the
purpose of sex is viewed as "drawing people from loneliness to relationship," as "mutuality," as "our belonging to
one another"; it has to do "with the human problem of
loneliness." If the whole problem is companionship and
relationship, etc., God could just as well have created
another human male, instead of a female, and brought

him to Adam. I do not think for a moment that this is
what the author wanted to say. Incidentally, the terms of
the law in Leviticus 18:22 are that "you shall not lie with
a (human) male as with a woman; it is abomination," the
penalty for that being death (Lv. 20:13).

The narrative in Genesis 2 and 3 forms a literary unit
of the Yahwist document and the narrative refers to the
"offspring" of the woman, to her pangs in child bearing,
to her desire for her husband (v. 15f.), and to Eve as "the
mother" of all the living (v. 20). The text refers to a relationship between a human male and a human female, to
the desire of a human female for a human male and to
motherhood and fatherhood. This is what human sexuality is for, according to the text of Genesis 2 (and 3). There
is more. The view of this text of Genesis expressed by the
Theological Society can be construed as a justification for
all kinds of sexual relations between men and women—it
is (they say) a matter of loneliness, mutuality, drawing
people from loneliness to relationship. Actually, this text
does not use the terms *zakar* (male) and *neqebah* (female)
as in Genesis 1:27. It uses the terms *ish* and *ishshah* that
in similar contexts connote the idea of husband and wife,
as the remainder of the narrative serves to prove when it
refers to "his/your" *ishshah* (wife) (2:24; 3:17, 20), to the
woman that "you (God) put in my company" (3:12), to
"her/your" *ish* (2:6; 3:16), and to the man "in her company" (2:6). It is a condition in which a man and a
woman are integrated into "one flesh"—one single human
living organism—are "bone and flesh" of each other, are
the "rib" and the rest of a total body; it is a condition in
which a man "leaves his father and mother" to adhere to
"his wife" (see Eph. 5:28f.: "one's own body, oneself,
one's own flesh"). In this perspective human sexuality
rather appears as the power that drives a human male
and a human female to integrate themselves into one
flesh; and this not necessarily by mating but by love
(dbq). The New Testament mentions the text of Genesis 2
within the framework of marriage and marital questions
(Mt. 19:5 parall.; Eph. 5:31).

Of course, this perspective of human sexuality in Genesis 2 (and 3) in no way conflicts with the perspective in Genesis 1 where God makes Adam—the human being —and Adam is multiple (that "they" may rule) but the multiplicity consists in this, namely, that "male and female he (God) created them." The human being— Adam—exists in two nuclei or polarities, both of them human, both of them complete in their nature of male and female—but neither can claim to be the complete human being, the complete Adam. The complete Adam exists when a male and a female integrate themselves into a *complete* Adam or total human organism. This is why in Genesis 1:27 Adam splits into male and female whereas in Genesis 5:3 (the same source P) a male plus a female add up to an Adam or total human organism. Again, human sexuality appears as the power that by its own nature brings two halves together in order to form the "whole" they are destined to integrate.

It is within this integrated whole that the power of procreation is pointed out as a "blessing." It is the biblical perspective that fecundity or fruitfulness is a gift or blessing added to the sexual maleness or femaleness of a human being. This is what the cases of sterile "women"— as such women or females—in the Bible serve to prove, as well as the fact that in the Bible children are regarded as a "blessing" or gift of God. Human sexuality can exist without fecundity. But everyday experience taught the biblical writers (as it teaches us today) that fruitfulness or fecundity, when it is given, is attached to human sexuality; human sexuality that drives a human male and human female to integrate themselves into the natural "oneness" of an Adam, which oneness, being natural, by its own nature is lasting and permanent. This is the understanding of this passage by the Lord in the Gospel (Mt. 19:5 parall.).

Obviously, there is no conflict between the passages of Genesis 1 and Genesis 2. It is the Lord Himself who puts them together (Mt. 19:4, 5) in His reference to the basis of a human marriage "from the beginning"; the author of Eph. 5:31f. follows His teaching. Each text presses a particular aspect, but the basic teaching is the same in both of them. In addition, in this as in all other matters, later revelation can develop earlier revelation and add to it. That is why the suggestion that "some four hundred years later (than Gn. 2), the Priestly tradition came to relate sexuality with procreation" is unwarranted. The relation of sexuality with procreation had already been established by the Yahwist and, before him, by common and universal experience. The specific point of the priestly writer is that the power of procreation—just as rule over earth and animals—is a gift or blessing added to the basic nature of mankind as male and female. In another direction it must be pointed out that, even if we could be sure that the Priestly writer composed his narrative about 555 B.C., we have to admit that the traditions incorporated into his work are much older. It can be as old as any other tradition in the Bible, the Yahwist not excluded.

Human Sexuality touches also, though slightly, upon another important text, namely, Genesis 38:9. It is maintained that the sin of Onan "was not simply the fact that he 'wasted his seed on the ground'.... The issue...was ostensibly one of justice...Onan was trying to steal his dead brother's inheritance" (p. 15).

Actually, what the text says is this: "Onan was aware that the offspring ("seed") would not be his; so when he went in unto his brother's wife he spilt *(shichet arzah;* LXX, *execheen:* he spoiled, perverted, corrupted to the ground) it on the ground, in order not to give offspring ("seed") to his brother. But what he did was evil in the sight of the Lord, and he (the Lord) slew him also."

It is clear that Onan spilt his seed on the ground in the awareness that the offspring would not be his and with the intention of not giving offspring to his brother. But it is *not* said in the text that this was the reason—or at least the *only* reason—why his deed was evil in the sight of the Lord. The text just says that what Onan did was evil—it could be evil for several reasons.

On the other hand, the question of "inheritance" is not mentioned in the text. It could be implied, but the solution is not that simple. Onan had another younger brother (Shelah) who had the same right and obligation to give children to his widowed sister-in-law; this is, in fact, what Judah, Onan's and Shelah's father, had in mind (v. 11). Onan could not be so sure of getting the inheritance of his dead brother (or even half of it). As far as we know, moreover, the widow could bring a case like Onan's to the law-court and claim the inheritance of her husband (Dt. 25:5-10). The example of Boaz and Ruth (in Ruth 4) shows that the husband's inheritance passed to his next of kin who married his widowed wife. It was not so sure that the inheritance of Onan's brother would come to him by not giving offspring to his brother. Another side of the question is that the simple transgression of the law (of levirate) had its specific penalty (Dt. 25:6-10).

In view of the fact that Judah intended to marry Shelah to Tamar (v. 11, 14b, 26), and in view of the understanding reflected in the seven brothers who successively took/married the same woman, the case of Onan seems well to be this: that he in fact married his brother's widow, but whenever he approached her he prevented her from conceiving (which she ardently wanted: see her trick to Judah himself for this purpose) by spilling his seed on the ground, the reason for this being that he did not want the line of his brother to continue. His concern was not so much for having children of his own (he could marry a second wife) but for denying children to his brother, which also frustrated the woman's desire for children.

The question is whether what was "evil in the Lord's sight" was Onan's purpose of denying children to his brother or the fact itself of wasting his own seed—or both. What Onan did is described in Hebrew by *shichet arzah* which is an unusual expression; in fact it is unique in the Old Testament. Our translations "he spilled (or wasted) it (the seed) on the ground" does not do complete justice to the Hebrew expression, precisely because the Hebrew verb (*shichet*) never means to spill or waste. The concept of spilling or wasting on the ground is certainly implied; this already was the understanding of the LXX (*execheen:* poured out). But the Hebrew verb denotes first of all a qualification or evaluation of this spilling or wasting. It is relevant to note that in this case (as in many others) the verb has no complement object; and an adverb of place accompanies the verb indicating the direction in which the action of the verb goes: *arzah*, to, towards, in the direction of the ground. Thus Onan *shichet* to the ground. Now the primary meaning of *shichet* is to corrupt. This is the same word that is used, v. gr., in the narrative of the Flood (Gn. 6:12) when "the Lord saw that the earth *was corrupt*, for all flesh has *corrupted* their way." Then, of course, the verb means "destroy" cities, walls, wisdom (Ez. 28:17), kings, etc. Importantly, however, when the meaning "to destroy" applies, the verb usually has a direct object (Nm. 35:15; Gn. 6:17; 13:10; 19:13, 29, etc.). There are many instances where, as in our passage, the verb has no direct object, and then it means to act *corruptly, perversely:* when the people in the desert set up the golden calf, they *shichet*, they acted (dealt) corruptly (Ex. 32:7; Dt. 9:12). With their serious sins the people of Ephraim *shichetu*, acted corruptly or perversely as in the days of Gibeah; God will remember their iniquity, He will punish their sins (Hos. 9:9). Once in possession of the promised land, "you (the people) *hishchatem* (no perceptible difference between *piel* and *hifil*) will act corruptly," and make idols and do what is evil in the sight of the Lord (Dt. 4:26); etc. In Psalm 14:1 "the fool has said in his heart 'there is no God'; they *hischitu*, acted corruptly; they have acted abominably; there is none who does good." The same thing and the same words are repeated in Psalm 53:2.

The grammatical feature (no object) and the usage of the language revealed by these and other examples seems to require for Onan's passage the understanding that, in order to attain his goal (no children for his brother), he "acted corruptly," perversely. But he did so *arzah*, towards the earth, ground; the action of the verb cannot be separated from this adverb. The text relates his perverse act to the ground, not to his brother (to act perversely *against* his brother). This turn of expression imposes the understanding and translation that "he acted perversely spilling his seed on the ground in order not to give offspring to his brother." It seems well that his perversion or corruption consists in his action itself, not precisely in the result and goal of his act. His intention was evil, but the means to that goal is itself corrupt or perverse. At any rate, in a strict interpretation the text says that what was evil in the sight of the Lord was what Onan actually did *(asher asah)*; the emphasis in this sentence of v. 10 does not fall on what he intended to achieve, but on what he "did."

Significant Omissions

As a third point in the treatment of the Old Testament in *Human Sexuality*, it must be emphasized that several passages relevant to the matter discussed are not even mentioned. Nothing is said about the implied criticism of Lamech because he was the first who took two wives (Gn. 4:19), about David's sin, about Amnon's affair with his half-sister, nothing about the important chapters 18 and 20 in Leviticus except the remark that they deal with the "taboo" of incest, nothing about the cause of the Flood in Genesis 6ff., where the author points out the "desires" in matter of sex, nothing about the relations between Lot and his daughters (Gn. 12), about Dinah's rape (Gn. 34), etc. Nothing is said about the faithfulness in marriage displayed by the prophet Hosea and about his high purpose of imitating in his marital union the covenantal relationship of a faithful Yahweh with an unfaithful Israel. The solemn statement of the prophet Malachi "I hate divorce, says Yahweh the God of Israel" (2:16) is not even mentioned. Of course, nothing is said about the principle "it was not so from the beginning."

Among the passages that are not even mentioned, that of the sin of Sodom and Gomorrah is certainly relevant. The reason for the omission probably is that homosexuality can be explained—so the authors of *Human Sexuality*, p. 10, think—by the ancient peoples' awe towards male seed; some sort of "taboo."

The scriptural text conveys a different impression. It is "an exceedingly grievous sin" (Gn. 18:23); as a matter of fact "the men of Sodom were wicked and sinners against the Lord exceedingly" (Gn. 13:13). In the biblical tradition Sodom and Gomorrah remain an example of wickedness and exemplary punishment (Jer. 23:24; Ez. 16:46ff.; Am. 4:11; Zep. 2:9; 2 Pt. 2:7; Jude 7). It is a matter of relating to the Lord, not to any impersonal power.

Was theirs a sin against hospitality? Whatever it is, as soon as they came to the town, Abraham's guests just at the "gate" of Sodom received Lot's invitation to lodge in his house, and he had to "urge them greatly" (v. 3), for they planned to spend the night in the town square (v. 2). Whatever happened came when they already were under a roof, had washed their feet, were treated to a feast, and were about to go to bed. The idea of lack of hospitality seems very foreign to the entire narrative. There is no indication that the people of the place came to Lot's house in order to send his guests away, precisely when they were about to go to bed, i.e., at night. It is not said, moreover, that Lot's guests ever went to Gomorrah, and yet it is destroyed for the same sin of Sodom. Incidentally, the author stresses that those who came to Lot's house were "the *men* of the town—men of Sodom" (v. 4), i.e., Sodomites; and whereas the guests are referred to as "angels" by the writer (v. 1), they are referred to as "men" (v. 5) by the "men of Sodom" who requested to see them.

The real nature of what is involved emerges from the dialogue between Lot and the "men of Sodom." These came to Lot's house and said to him: "where (not 'who') are the men that came to you tonight? Bring them out to us that we may know them. Lot went out to them at the entrance, shut the door behind him, and said: I beg you, my brothers, do not do wickedly...I have two (virgin) daughters...do to them as you please; only do not do anything to these *men*, for they have come under the shelter of my roof. But they said: stand back!...we will deal worse with you than with them." The punishment follows.

The key to a correct understanding lies in the request of the men in town: they want to "know" the male guests. What they want is not that the guests be "introduced" to them as a matter of politeness or public relations. In their wish to "know," Lot sees something sinister, for he begs them not to do *wickedly*. They are wicked-minded; it is a wicked "knowledge" that is involved; which, in turn, explains why Lot shut the door behind him. Furthermore, Lot understands that the wicked "knowledge" in their minds involves sexual activity. Only this can be the reason why Lot tries to appease them by offering his own daughters to them, at the same time that he asks them to use the women but not the "men"—the contrast between the daughters and the men is only obvious. It was Lot's understanding that the "men" had to serve the same general purpose that women do. In the existing narrative nothing happens to the women either. But the strange offer of Lot intends to emphasize the real inclination of the men in town: they refuse women and look for men in order to "know them." In this context "knowing" can't but express the notion of sexual intimacy, which is usual in the biblical language.

The parallel passage in Judges 19 and 20 adds something to the episode of Sodom, without changing anything in the nature of the sin. In Judges the "evil men" (19:22) wanted to "know" the man (v. 22), but they were offered his concubine and they "knew" her and abused her until she died. This is why the man then explains that "it was me they meant to kill, but it was my concubine that they raped and she is dead" (20:5). Unless this is an exaggeration of the man, the suggestion seems to be that the wicked men intended to kill the guest by "knowing" him, as they did with his concubine. This may be an offense against hospitality, but it is a qualified one: it is not just a "vile act," it is also *zimmah*, a "shameful deed," which is usually said of impure actions (Lv. 18:17; 19:29; 20:14; Ez. 16:27, 43, 58, etc.); it is lewdness.

In both cases the severe punishment that follows shows that the offense is truly serious. Gibeah also remained in the biblical tradition an example of legendary corruption (Hos. 9:9; 10:9).

CHAPTER THREE

Sexuality and Marriage
in the Teaching of the Church

Rev. Robert I. Bradley, S.J.

If any one topic and event of the past decade were to be selected from among the many which have been called "signs of the times," as most appropriately fulfilling the sense of that Biblical and Conciliar expression,[1] there should be little doubt as to what that topic and event would be. The topic would be "sexuality and marriage"; and the event would be the Encyclical Letter of Pope Paul VI, *Humanae vitae*. For, if what the Gospel and the Council meant by a "sign of the times" something unmistakably and prophetically momentous to human destiny, then what the Holy Father said—and how he said it—in that encyclical is a "sign of the times" clearer than all others. *Humanae vitae* has been ignored, as perhaps no other encyclical has ever been. Yet it is not, and cannot be, forgotten. Clearly it is, for good or ill, *the* "sign of our times."

Since the tenth anniversary of *Humanae vitae* prompted the selection of the general topic of this series, I would like to preface my presentation on the specific topic assigned me, "Sexuality and Marriage in the Teaching of the Church," with two remarks, in the interest of precision and of fidelity to the encyclical.

As my first remark I would like to reword the title to a slight degree: for the word "sexuality" I would substitute the word "sex." I know, "sexuality" probably sounds better. But I must forego that possible advantage if my presentation is to follow the same general lines as Pope Paul's. "Sexuality" connotes more than "sex." It includes all the complementary qualities of human nature and personality as differentiated by "masculine" and "feminine." Such issues, for instance, as the so-called "women's liberation" movement (at least in most of its facets)—not to mention the radical issue of homosexuality which would negate the very basis of this differentiation—all such issues are foreign to *Humanae vitae*, except insofar, of course, as they are implied as inevitable consequences to the disregarding of the Encyclical's teaching. For our present discussion, therefore, the word "sex" is more appropriate. For that word denotes "male" and "female" rather than "masculine" and "feminine," the physiological rather than the psychological. "Sex" concerns the physical use, in thought or deed, of the power and instinct called "sexuality."

As a second prefatory remark I would like to comment briefly on the phrase "what the Church teaches." In *Humanae vitae* Paul VI did more than simply invoke the authority of his office in expounding a matter of faith or morals. This, of course, clearly and principally is what he did. But he also "theologized" in the strict sense of that term; he sought by reasoning to make more intelligible the data of the faith. This secondary function of the Encyclical involved some risk. Giving reasons *why* the Church teaches *what* she teaches might induce some Catholics to consider only those reasons, and if they are not convinced by those reasons, they then consider themselves free from the obligation of the "obedience of faith." Such a conclusion betrays, of course, a complete ignorance of what faith really is; and that conclusion, as we now well know, has been made by all too many Catholics in these past ten years. That risk, was, however, worth running, because theologizing involves a process of reasoning which is also suited to data not included in the faith as such, and which therefore does not necessarily presuppose the faith. Now, *Humanae vitae* was clearly not limited to the faithful alone. It was an exercise of the teaching office of the Church regarding the moral law as such, and as such it could be—and was in fact—directed to all men. The reasoning was thus grounded in realities which can be attained and verified apart from revelation; and reasonings of this kind can be guaranteed by the Church's charism of infallibility even in her extraordinary magisterium—as, for instance, in the First Vatican Council's solemn definition regarding the natural knowability of the existence and perfections of God.[2]

What is of faith and what is of reason are thus just as intimately connected in the Church's teaching as they are in the human mind that receives that teaching; for it is, after all, the same mind that we use when we supernaturally believe and when we naturally perceive. "Grace builds on nature," it is said; and if faith and reason thus stand together, the rejection of one can well lead to the rejection of both.[3] That this relationship has been verified in the case of *Humanae vitae*—and of the Church's entire body of teaching on sex and marriage—can be demonstrated negatively by noting what has happened to the autonomy of reason in a culture whose faith has been lost. Instead of treating sex as something that can be understood only as a constituent or instrument of something apart from and above itself, our modern secular culture now sees sex as something strictly autonomous: a power and an instinct which is self-contained and self-explaining. Only now—as should be evident to anyone—its self-explanation is no explanation, and its self-containedness is no continence. The intelligibility of sex unto itself is insanity, and the harmony of sex unto itself is chaos.

If negatively the denial or disregard of the Church's teaching leads to a dead end of intellect in this matter, positively that teaching leads to its illumination. This positive intelligibility of sex and marriage, as taught by the Church, can for convenience's sake be summarized in the following brief formula or "thesis": "Sex is for marriage, and marriage is for Christ."

The body of this presentation, following my two prefatory remarks, will be simply a commentary on the two successive parts of this thesis. Let us proceed with the first part: "Sex is for marriage."

Despite some breathless revelations from modern psychologists probing into the mating habits of rats, the fact is that the so-called "facts of life" as applied to human life must have been sufficiently well known from the beginning of mankind—otherwise, mankind would not have survived its beginning! Until our own times, it seems, the mechanics of coition and reproduction was seen as just that: mechanics. What was awesome and indeed breathless was the *significance* of this mechanism and action as something *human*. Sex was seen not so much as a fact in itself as, rather, a fact leading us to recognize in it a further fact, one higher and deeper than itself. That further reality is also a fact; but it is not immediate and material, and so it remains elusive, especially after man's original sin impaired the order of all his actions because of his darkened understanding and weakened will. But this human debilitation, profound and comprehensive as it is, does not extinguish man's specific nature as an essentially spiritual and immortal being. And so there remains the "intimations of immortality"; and nowhere are these intimations more intimate than in the intimacy of sex. What a thrill man feels—at once fearful and fascinating—that into flesh should descend his yearnings for a deathless love, and that out of this same flesh should arise the stirrings of a new deathless life.

Although it is thus clearly helpful to have the Church's solemn teaching on original sin—especially as enunciated in the great Tridentine canons[4]—as a first and fundamental premise to a true understanding of sex, it is not strictly necessary. For it is a fact firmly established by mere empirical observation that sex has always and everywhere been regarded as something "special" to man, in the literal sense of being *specific* to him. It is specifically human because it combines the animality of its *sign* with the spirituality of its *significance*. By the former it excludes the angels; by the latter it excludes the brutes. The empirical fact is that in all historic cultures the *use* of sex has always been *limited* in some manner. The limitations (or "taboos," if you will) have varied widely, it is true: from such minimal limitations as incest or bestiality, on up to the detailed strictures of elaborated societies (which societies, incidentally, are by no means to be equated with those which are more materially advanced). Moreover, this invariable limitation on the use of sex is invariably connected with a sense of the *sacred*. The sacredness may be manifested in ways as varied as the limitations themselves. But the sacred in *some* sense is always there, even if, as in our modern secular culture, the "sacredness" survives only in its counterfeit: the apotheosized profanity, the idolized blasphemy, the worshipped abomination in the desecrated sanctuary of this modern, sick world of ours.

Now, among all the historic limitations and sacred sanctionings regarding sex, and as it were fulfilling them, stands the teaching of the Catholic Church. It is interesting to note that her teaching on sex was never codified in solemn canons, such as for instance the teaching already referred to on original sin and justifying grace. It is as though this matter of sex were so immediate and pervasive in the lives of her children that the more appropriate form of her teaching concerning it would itself be the immediate and pervasive form we call the ordinary and universal magisterium. Yet this ordinary magisterium does look back to an extraordinary and unique occasion, viz., when the teaching authority of God Himself was officially committed in the promulgation of the Decalogue by Moses on Mt. Sinai. The Sixth Commandment, "You shall not commit adultery," and the Ninth Commandment, "You shall not covet your neighbor's wife," constitute the first formal statement of revealed truth regarding the use of sex.[5] This revelation confirmed the antecedent instinctive reasonings of human nature, for the limitation it now sets is definitive: sex is to be used only in marriage. And this limitation is now sanctioned by supreme sacred law. The Church has in her turn made these two Commandments of God the summation of her ordinary and universal teaching on the use of sex, because these Commandments were carried over without change into the New Testament by Christ Himself.[6] Our Lord did indeed add new Commandments, but only in order to fulfill more perfectly the old.[7] As we shall see in the second part of this presentation, the Church's teaching that "marriage is for Christ" is but the fulfillment of the radical finality of what she inherited from the Old Law, viz., the teaching that "sex is for marriage."

Before we proceed to this second part of our "thesis," however, it may be well to note that this ordinary and universal magisterium can be singled out in specific instances right across the history of the Church. Thus, masturbation was explicitly condemned as early as the 11th century,[8] and mutilation as early as the 12th.[9] The teaching that fornication—and by implication all the other forms of "uncleanness" associated with it in the New Testament—is always a mortal sin was declared as early as the 13th century.[10] And by the 17th century it was clearly stated as a guiding principle for confessors that the matter in the case of all sins against the Sixth and Ninth Commandments is always grave.[11] Finally, of course, we have most recently, in 1975, the Declaration of the Sacred Congregation for the Doctrine of the Faith categorically reaffirming the Church's teaching on the sinfulness of all pre-marital and extra-marital sex.[12] Thus, in conclusion, this first part of our "thesis"—"sex is for marriage"—simply means that sex is a reality that does not exist for itself, and therefore does not explain itself. Rather, it is a reality that has the essential nature of a sign; and what it *signifies* is marriage. Only in marriage is sex permissible, because only in marriage is sex intelligible. Both the instinct of reason and the revelation of faith converge in this one absolute truth: without marriage sex is literally inhuman; but within marriage sex can be instrumentally divine.

We can now proceed to the second part of our "thesis": "marriage is for Christ."

As we have seen, the Church's teaching that sex is essentially ordered to marriage was historically derived from the Old Law under Judaism. But the Church proceeded to refine the Judaic prescriptions regarding marriage, because Christ, while explicitly retaining the Commandments, just as explicitly rejected some of the prescriptions that had grown up around them.[13] Thus, under the Old Law the observance of the Sixth Commandment was compatible with polygamous marriage—whether the polygamy was simultaneous or successive. To this observance Christ answered: not so. Pointing to the very first passages of their own Scriptures, Christ showed Israel that marriage as an institution is something absolutely unique; it was not dependent on any earthly law, even the Law of Moses.[14] It preceded all earthly laws, for it came directly from God. Indeed, all laws on earth—even the Law mediated by Moses—were dependent on *it*. All covenants were modelled on *this* covenant: the divinely instituted covenant of marriage, in which God Himself joins man and woman into one exclusive and indissoluble society. This society stands as the source and base of all other human societies; and without it, they cannot naturally exist.

Such was the true natural status of marriage in the judgment of Christ; and to this status, by His authority as Son of Man, He restored it. That original true status was comprised of two values. The first value, narrated in the first chapter of Genesis, is *fruitfulness* ("increase and multiply...");[15] and the second value, narrated in the second chapter of Genesis, is *faithfulness* ("a man shall leave father and mother and cleave to his wife, and they shall become one flesh").[16] Just as it is obvious that sex as a function serves both values, it is equally obvious that both values utterly transcend sex. Together they constitute the one integral value called marriage, than which no higher natural value can be conceived.

This truth of marriage as first taught by Christ our Lord in His Gospel and as witnessed to by His Church in her magisterium, applies to *all* marriages without exception. Upon all mankind, therefore, falls the same one injunction of the law of God, a law which is at once natural and positive, viz., that only that sexual union is true marriage in which one man and one woman freely consent to a mutual bodily donation and possession which is exclusive and permanent, for the purpose of begetting and raising offspring and for their own mutual love and assistance. You will notice the perfect harmonization here of the respective claims of *nature* and *person*. Marriage as such, in its nature, is not made by the persons being married; much less is it made by the state, or even by the Church, or by any other person or persons. It is made only by God, originally in Paradise and now renewed in the union of this man and this woman. At the same time, however, *this* marriage here and now *is* being made by the persons being married, in the sense that each of the two is freely and fully consenting, first, to enter the marriage state itself (with its two-fold value of fecundity and fidelity), and second, to enter it with *this* person as spouse. In this personal consent—at once individual and mutual—and in nothing else, consists the essence of any true marriage.

As I mentioned at the beginning of this presentation, our "thesis" consists of two parts. The first part—"sex is for marriage"—has been, I should hope, sufficiently explained. It was summarized, you will remember, by our saying that sex has its meaning, its finality, its intelligibility, its significance only in marriage. Then we came to the second part: "marriage is for Christ." But have we as yet really presented this second and analogous truth: that marriage has *its* meaning, its finality, its intelligibility, its significance only in Christ? No, we have not. So far we have seen our Lord only as the sovereign

Judge of that natural institution as created by His Father. We have, as it were, seen marriage only as Christ *found* it. We have not as yet seen it as He *founded* it. For the *natural* value of marriage, supreme in the order of nature as it is, was still immeasurably beneath the value that Christ brought in His Person into the human race.

That new value is simply the divine life itself; and that by which it subsists in the creature is called *grace*. In one respect, of course, the grace of Christ is incommunicable, for it is identified with the Sacred Humanity itself; and in this respect it is called the "grace of union" which made possible the Incarnation. But in another respect the grace of Christ is most communicable, for there is no grace anywhere in creation which is not *His*. In this sense His grace is called the "grace of headship," for it is meant to be shared, to form a total body around and under Him. This reality of Christ's grace, this value of the divine life, was not effectively manifested and communicated until His death and resurrection. Before then, and indeed from the very beginning of mankind, it was *hidden*. St. Paul's Letter to the Ephesians stresses both the hiddenness then and the manifestness now; both are facets of the same one reality; they comprise the *musterion:* the "Mystery" of Christ.[17]

Now, what has all this to do with marriage? you may ask. It has everything to do with it! For St. Paul in this very same letter goes on to identify this "Mystery" with—marriage.[18] Marriage was formerly the hidden, and now it is the manifest *musterion* or *sacramentum* or "sign" (all three words are synonyms) of Christ's grace as shared with His creature, the grace by which He the Bridegroom and the Church His Bride become two in one flesh to form one Body. So real is *this* Marriage—this marriage by which Christ fulfills Himself in total faithfulness and fruitfulness with His Bride—that in comparison with *it* all purely natural human marriages are but its *sign!* They lack their full meaning, their full finality, their full intelligibility, without Him. That is what we mean when we say: "marriage is for Christ."

Christian marriage is thus the divinization of natural marriage, analogously to the manner in which natural marriage is the humanization of sex. To pursue this analogy, it would be a mistake to suppose that the sacramentality of marriage is something *added* to a marriage otherwise constituted, as though the sacrament consisted merely in a blessing by the Church on a contract already made. On the contrary, the Church teaches that the actual consent to marry by two baptized persons legitimately able to give such consent is ipso facto the sacrament.[19] The consequences of this indissolubility between the contract and the sacrament are more than merely theoretical. It justifies—indeed, it necessitates—the role of the Church as the witness and guardian of Christian marriage. Moreover, it preserves intact the two-fold value of fruitfulness and faithfulness (or fecundity and fidelity) that we have seen as being essential to the married state. Only now, it adds as it were a third value—*sacramentality*—by which the other two are supernaturalized: begetting and raising children into the divine life, and pledging a mutual assistance for growing into the divine love.[20] This new third value of sacramentality is neither a *substitution* for the other two, nor is it a *juxtaposition* alongside them. To affirm the former is equivalently to be a Monophysite; to affirm the later is equivalently to be a Nestorian. No, just as Christ Himself is true God and true Man in one divine Person, so His sacrament of marriage—the sign of His life and love with the Church—is at once fully divine and fully human in the one sacred covenant of His founding.

This continuity which we have drawn (or rather, which St. Paul has drawn, for we are but paraphrasing him) between the Reality of the total Christ and the Mystery of His union with the Church, which both hides and manifests that Reality, and the equation of that Mystery with Christian marriage—all this truly tremendous teaching of the Church may perhaps incline us to absolutize this sacrament into something beyond what it really is as intended by our Lord. I am referring to the

temptation about which Pius XII warned us in his Encyclical *Sacra virginitas*, viz., the view that marriage is
the highest—if indeed it is not the only—authentic Christian vocation, and that the renunciation of marriage is
therefore an aberration, a selfishness offending both
nature and grace.[21] It should suffice simply to recall that
the same Apostle who wrote to the Ephesians wrote
earlier to the Corinthians that virginity for the sake of
Christ was clearly preferable to marriage[22]; and in this
teaching he was but making explicit the teaching of
Christ Himself.[23] Why is sacred virginity superior as a
state of life to sacred marriage? Because the sign that constitutes marriage—the mutual consent to a mutual bodily
donation and possession—is essentially temporal; whereas the sign that consecrates virginity—the offering of
one's total self, body and soul, to become "one spirit"
with the Lord—is essentially eternal. There will be no
marrying nor giving in marriage in heaven, for the children of the resurrection will be like the angels.[24] And so
virginity, which anticipates by grace this final state of the
faithful Christian, is superior to marriage. And that is
also why marriage as a sacrament, for all its indissolubility, does not impart an indelible sacramental seal, as do
Baptism, Confirmation and Orders.[25] The married state
endures "until death do us part"; but the priestly state—
whether that which is common to all the baptized or that
which is special and ministerial—is "in aeternum."

And yet—and yet the fundamental unity of the total
Christian life remains true, just as He, Jesus, is but the
one Christ. If, therefore, on the one hand it is true that
earthly sacramental marriage is but a mediate way to the
attainment of the life of the angels, it is on the other hand
equally true that that very life of heaven has been compared by our Lord Himself—and more than once—to a
wedding feast![26] We will not *become* angels in heaven;
we will only be *like* them! Our bodies—and that means
our sexuality—will be risen and with the Lord in His
Body.

This vision before us—this blessed vision of peace, of the new heaven and the new earth, where we are Christ's and Christ is God's and God is all in all—this vision is not some pious imagining of ours, and thus some departure from the task assigned us. No, this vision is the clear, emphatic vision of *faith*, as revealed in the Sacred Scriptures and interpreted and proclaimed by the Magisterium of the Catholic Church. This Magisterium has been referred to several times earlier in this presentation; and already we have had occasion to note certain aspects of its exercise on this general topic of sex and marriage, which have remained characteristic of the Church right down to our times, and are particularly significant now, as being indeed a "sign of the times." One such aspect was the "ordinariness" of the Magisterium in this area: its being so "occasional," even so casual. Yet the complementary aspect must not be overlooked: its being so matter-of-fact, even so emphatic. This truly significant combination of sobriety and certainty, of letting the tradition speak for itself and articulating the tradition whenever it was persistently challenged, of stressing now one, now another of the manifold values of her moral doctrine, and maintaining them all in the perfect harmony of their one source and their one finality—all this, I say, has been the lived experience of the Church from the very beginning. But now, in this latest century of her history, this providential complementarity, this balance and dynamism, in her Magisterium has achieved a greatness, a prominence that makes it truly a "sign of the times." Let me offer you now, as the final part of this presentation, a brief résumé of the teaching of the Church on the specific topic of marriage.

Although we are limiting ourselves to the last hundred years, we must nevertheless include that extraordinary Magisterial moment without which nothing in the subsequent history of the Magisterium is really understandable. I am referring to the great Council of Trent, which left on the doctrine of marriage—as on that of all the Sacraments—its indelible mark. In its 24th (and penultimate) session (in 1563) the Council issued 12 Canons, in which (among other, lesser matters) were solemnly defined: the sacramentality of Christian marriage,[27] its properties of unity[28] and indissolubility,[29] and the competence of the Church to adjudicate its conditions and circumstances.[30] As in all the other areas of doctrine which it touched, so thorough was the Tridentine teaching that there has as yet been no need for further exercise of the extraordinary Magisterium on the doctrine of marriage. As for the ordinary Magisterium, there have been four outstanding statements by it over the last hundred years.

First, there was the Encyclical *Arcanum Divinae Sapientiae* of Leo XIII in 1880.[31] Pope Leo did not intend a complete review and summary of the Church's teaching on marriage. Although he does explicitly reiterate its sacramentality, unity and indissolubility, and although he also affirms the essential equality of husband and wife as persons, and the twofold value of procreation and mutual love, these points are but incidental to the main purpose of the Encyclical, which was to assert, against the pretensions of the then emerging totally secular state, identification of the sacrament with the contract in every Christian marriage, and consequently the necessarily primary jurisdiction of the Church regarding Christian marriages. Leo went on to condemn in particular one of the results of the unjust interference of the state, viz., the new laws relaxing the traditional prohibition of divorce. He prophesied that this liberalization would lead to a state of affairs where the natural interests of the state would be just as much weakened as the supernatural interests of the Church.

Fifty years later, in 1930, came the most comprehensive and eloquent statement on marriage in the entire history of the Church, Pius XI's incomparable *Casti connubii*.[32] This Encyclical is divided into three parts of approximately equal length. In the first part Pope Pius repeats the teaching of Trent and Leo XIII on its nature and properties by developing the classic tripartite value

(bonum) of Christian marriage, as first enunciated by
St. Augustine and as reviewed earlier in this presentation,
viz.: the child *(proles)*, mutual love *(fides)* and the indissoluble bond *(sacramentum)*.[33] He develops all three
of these values by positing new emphases on each of
them: procreation of children must include their education; mutual love of the spouses means a mutual complementarity of husband and wife; and the indissoluble
bond admits of degrees culminating in the supreme instance of the sacrament *ratum et consummatum*. Pro-
ceeding then to the second part of his Encyclical Pius XI
exposes the errors of the times, all stemming radically
from the denial of the divine institution of marriage both
in nature and in grace, and all leading ultimately to the
denial of marriage as even a human institution. Contraception (which is given primacy of place and emphasis
undoubtedly because of the recent Anglican statement,
which is referred to without being named), abortion,
sterilization, and divorce are successively and formally
condemned. Finally, in the third part, he concludes the
Encyclical with a positive and pastoral exhortation: to
careful instruction and encouragement in all these matters on the part of the clergy, to the integration of this
knowledge and pastoral help within their total Catholic
life on the part of all married people, to prudent and
prayerful preparation for marriage on the part of the
young, to responsible cooperation with families and with
the Church on the part of the State.

The third great statement in our list differs from the
preceding two in that it has not a Pope but a Council for
its author. I am referring, of course, to the Second
Vatican Council's teaching on marriage, which it incorporated as Chapter I in Part II of its Pastoral Constitution
on the Church in Our Times *Gaudium et spes*, promulgated in 1965.[34] This Conciliar statement, however,
fits integrally into the sequence of the Papal statements,
for it intended neither merely to repeat them (which was
unnecessary) nor, obviously, to repeal them (which was

impossible), but rather to *develop* them. In fact, Vatican II's development of Pius XI is in some ways reminiscent of Pius' development of Leo XIII. What was progressively developed in both was the doctrine of "personalism": the emphasis on the *human person* as the *one* value immediately and inalienably involved in both the communicative and the generative aspects (corresponding to the fidelity and the fecundity) of marriage. With this increased awareness of personalism as the "common denominator" of marriage values, it is no surprise that the Council carefully avoided the old terminology of "primary" and "secondary ends" in marriage. Both their respective individual realities and their profound mutuality were described—and documented—in no less than five explicit references to *Casti connubii*.[35] This is undoubtedly one of the real achievements of *Gaudium et spes*, that—for all its admitted "wordiness" and accommodation to sometimes sharply opposing points of view among the Council Fathers—it was actually able to perfect the consummate greatness of the teaching of Pius XI.

But if Vatican II thus built upon and furthered the work of the preceding Popes, it was in turn to be built upon and furthered—as it itself had already clearly anticipated—by the Pope who presided over it and promulgated its documents: Paul VI. His Encyclical *Humanae vitae*, issued in 1968, is the fourth and last in our magisterial series.[36] It is surely unnecessary to repeat *its* teaching as something not yet sufficiently known! But what may be worth noting here is its fidelity, not to the total Tradition in general (that is obvious, even to its opponents) but to the immediate tradition in particular of the Council itself. For all that Pope Paul really does in *Humanae vitae* is simply draw the inevitable conclusion from the premises declared in *Gaudium et spes*. The Council had made explicit what was but implicit in the previous teaching, viz., the *de jure indivisibility* of the two values—communion and generation, fidelity and fecundity, love and life. The Holy Father only makes the further explicitation that these two values must not there-fore be *deliberately separated de facto* in the marriage act.

These four statements, then—*Arcanum divinae, Casti connubii, Gaudium et spes,* and *Humanae vitae*—form the cumulative corpus of the Church's teaching on marriage. Their remarkable unity and mutual coherence, while at the same time their striking individuality and diversity, suggest a daring analogy which I offer you now with all due reserve. We may perhaps find more clearly in them the divine Providence which is surely there if we were to compare them to the four Gospels. In Leo XIII we have St. Matthew: juridical, ecclesial, stressing the in-stitution and the societal nature of things. In Pius XI we see St. Mark: where the Master speaks both roundly and right to the point, and His authority is most vividly manifest by His exorcising demons. In Vatican II we have St. Luke: the dear Physician, treating with nuance and compassion the poor and the pagans waiting for the Church. And lastly with Paul VI we have St. John: com-pounding the total Gospel paradox of the Incarnation—the eagle, at once so imperial and so vulnerable.

Our analogy limps, of course, on many counts; first of all because we do not have in our four documents that inspiration in the strict sense that the Holy Spirit has reserved uniquely to His Scriptures. But not least of all because neither do we have in these four documents, even on the level of human authorship, a completed Canon. No, the magisterium will go on till the end of time, declaring—ordinarily or even extraordinarily as the occa-sion requires—the unchanging doctrine of the Church. Even after *Humanae vitae*, in fact, we have heard again the voice of the teaching Church, most notably in the Declaration *Persona humana* of 1975.[37] We have already referred to this statement earlier in our presentation; and the reason why we do not include it here in our résumé on marriage is that its scope was more general. It concerned "Sexual Ethics," a topic proper to the first half of our discussion.

This explicit return by the magisterium to formal teaching on sexual morality in general—i.e., in matters regarding sex apart from and antecedent to the morality of marriage in particular—is itself a most significant development, truly a "sign of the times"! *and* a literal fulfillment of Pope Paul's prophecy in *Humanae vitae*. If one denies or ignores the teaching in that Encyclical, one has in effect denied marriage itself, and so has destroyed the continuum of nature and grace in this most intimate area of human life. It is literally the *death wish* that we are witnessing; and its most eloquent statement is, undoubtedly, the vaunted study of the American Catholic Theological Society on "Human Sexuality."[38] This monument to our new self-appointed "American Catholic" magisterium can be fairly summarized as saying "Sex is for Christ"—and never mind about marriage. Which is more despicable is hard to say: its intellectual shabbiness (its sin against reason) or its moral posturing (its sin against grace). It talks of "love," of course, of "creativity" and "integration" and many another cliché of this decadent age. But they are mere words, pathetic incantations in the night, husks of a vanished reason and faith. For the *real* meaning in the murk of this "study" is not that "Sex is for Christ" but that "Christ is for sex." And this inversion —this blasphemous perversion—is its real summary, its "sign of the times."

We began this presentation by saying that *Humanae vitae*, both in its message and in its reception, is the one great "sign of the times" in which we live. From both the continuity and the crescendo that we have now seen in that message and in its reception, there is little danger of our exaggerating its significance. That the contemporary crisis of faith, and its concomitant crisis of reason, should have been occasioned by this crisis concerning sex and marriage is in itself a truly apocalyptic sign. For what is at issue is *human life* itself. Human life—from its source in sex, through its mediation in marriage, to its consummation in beatitude—is itself the "sign" of the continuum of God's Providence: the continuum which can be summarized by saying once and for all that "sex is for marriage, and marriage is for Christ."

Notes

1. For "signs of the times" in the Gospels, cf. Mt. 24, Mk. 13, Lk. 21; in the Second Vatican Council, cf. *Gaudium et spes*, no. 4; *Dignitatis humanae*, no. 15, *Unitatis redintegratio*, no. 4.

2. DS 3004, 3026.

3. As it was in many other respects concerning the century that followed it, the First Vatican Council was singularly prophetic in the way it juxtaposed its condemnations of both Rationalism and Fideism. It is impossible to deny that the present crisis in the Church is as much a crisis of reason as it is a crisis of faith. The only question here that is really debatable is the precise causal relationship between them: which crisis came first?

4. DS 1510-15.

5. Ex. 20:14, 17; Dt. 5:18, 21.

6. Cf. Mt. 19:17-19; Mk. 10:19; Lk. 18:20.

7. Cf. Jn. 13:34.

8. St. Leo IX, in a letter to St. Peter Damian, 1054 (DS 687-88).

9. Lucius III, in a letter to the bishop of Meaux, c. 1183 (DS 762).

10. Innocent IV, in a letter to the bishop of Tusculum, 1254 (DS 835).

11. No. 48 of the 65 Propositions condemned by the Holy Office, 1679 (DS 2148).

12. *Persona humana*, Dec. 29, 1975 (*AAS* 48:77-96).

13. Cf. Mt. 15:3; Mk. 7:8.

14. Mt. 19:8; Mk. 10:5-6.

15. Gn. 1:28.

16. Gn. 2:24.

17. Eph. 3:3-5.

18. Eph. 5:31-32.

19. Syllabus of Errors, no. 66; Dec. 8, 1864 (DS 2966). This teaching was repeated with emphasis by Leo XIII in his Encyclical *Arcanum divinum sapientiae* (DS 3145). Cf. *infra*, footnote 31.

20. Cf. Pius XI's Encyclical *Casti connubii* (DS 3703ff.). Cf. *infra*, footnote 32.

21. DS 3911.

22. 1 Cor. 7:25-38.

23. Mt. 19:11-12.

24. Mt. 22:30; Mk. 12:25; Lk. 20:35-36.

25. Pius XI, in *Casti connubii* (*AAS* 22:555), compares marriage with these other sacraments, and says that the permanence of marriage is operative "almost in the same way" as that of the others.

26. Mt. 22:2; cf. Apoc. 19:9.

27. Canon 1 (DS 1801).

28. Canon 2 (DS 1802).

29. Canons 5 and 7 (DS 1805, 07).

30. Canons 3, 4, and 12 (DS 1803, 04, 12).

31. *AAS* 12:385-402. This Encyclical is included in practically all the standard collections in English of Leo XIII's major works.

32. *AAS* 22:539-592. This Encyclical is readily available in translation in any of the standard collections of Pius XI's major works. Moreover unlike *Arcanum* of Leo XIII, it has been frequently republished in pamphlet form (e.g., Daughters of St. Paul, St. Paul Editions, Boston).

33. Cf. *supra*, footnote 20.

34. *AAS* 43:1067-74. For an English translation, cf. Austin Flannery, O.P., *Vatican Council II: The Conciliar and Post-Conciliar Documents* (Northport, NY: Costello, 1975), pp. 949-57.

35. *Gaudium et spes*, no. 48, footnotes 1 and 2 (Flannery, p. 950) and 7 (p. 951); no. 49, footnote 11 (p. 952); no. 51, footnote 14 (p. 955).

36. *AAS* 40:481-503. Regarding English translations, cf. *supra*, footnote 32.

37. Cf. *supra*, footnote 12.

38. Anthony Kosnik, et. al., *Human Sexuality: New Directions in American Catholic Thought.* A study commissioned by the Catholic Theological Society of America, New York: Paulist Press, 1977.

CHAPTER FOUR

Sex and Sanctity

Rev. John A. Hardon, S.J.

The first reaction to a subject like sex and sanctity is wonder or misgiving. We have become so accustomed to associate sex with sin that even our vocabulary has been affected by the association. The first thought that comes to most people's minds on hearing words like impurity or immorality is some failure against chastity, as though there was something inherently wrong with the use of the sexual faculties, or as though the essence of evil was sin against the sixth and ninth commandments of the Decalogue.

I think there is some explanation for this unwarranted connection between sex and sin in the Manichaean virus that first infected the stream of Christianity in the third and fourth centuries, that became a major heresy in Europe, as Albigenseanism in the thirteenth century, that re-entered Western society under Calvin and Jansenius, and that still deeply affects large segments of Euro-American culture today.

My purpose in the present conference is not to disprove Manichaean dualism, which postulates that matter, and therefore the human body, is evil. I wish rather to show that, as Catholic Christianity understands the body and the functions of the organs of reproduction, sex is a creature that, in God's providence, is intended to help mankind reach not only their eternal destiny but to become holy. It is not as though we can be saved in spite of sex, but sex is a divinely instituted means of achieving our salvation, in fact our sanctification.

The stress in my presentation, therefore, is on sex as a means, and sanctity as the end. I assume that sanctity is achieved by doing the will of God according to one's state of life; and sex is an inevitable part of everyone's state of life. Sex is inescapable, sanctity is attainable. And a major factor in attaining sanctity depends on how a person copes with sex in his or her particular state of life.

For the sake of convenience, I will distinguish three general states of life in each of which sex is divinely intended to be a means of sustaining and growing in the life of God.

There is the state of marriage; the single state in the world; and the state of consecrated celibacy.

In what follows, I plan to deal with each of these three in terms of sex that I will call
—Sex as experience
—Sex as temperance and
—Sex as sacrifice.

Sex As Experience

Since the origins of Christianity, the Church has uniformly held that Christian marriage is holy. It is moreover not only sacred because instituted by God as the Author of nature and human society. It is a sacrament because instituted by the Son of God as the Author of grace and of the supernatural society which is the Church.

But marriage is not only holy in its origins. It is also holy in its purpose. This purpose is to sanctify husband and wife and, through them, the children they may bring into the world. Since sex is an essential part of marriage, it stands to reason (and faith) that the experience of sex is also part of the sanctifying purpose of marriage.

Since all the faithful are called to holiness, it is only to be expected that the married faithful are to become holy too. Their experience of sex within marriage must be one of the divinely-appointed means of becoming holy.

How so? How is the experience of sex sanctifying? It is sanctifying as joy, as charity, as restraint and as generosity.

1. Sexual experience is sanctifying as joy because the intense satisfaction associated with the marital act is intended by God to be enjoyed. Enjoyment is sanctifying insofar as the pleasure experience is accepted with gratitude from the Almighty and received from Him as a gift of His bounty.

After all, we are sanctified by every conscious act we perform according to the will of God. The more noble the act, the more it contributes to our sanctification. Who would doubt that marital intercourse is a noble action, or that properly performed it is pleasing to God. What pleases God sanctifies man, which means that by their "coming together," as the biblical phrase has it, husband and wife grow in the divine life in their souls through the loving union of their bodies.

2. Sexual experience is sanctifying as charity because by it the married spouses express their mutual love. We are to love one another, as Christ told us; and loving one another means showing this affection not only in words but also and especially in deeds.

By their marital embrace, the husband tells his wife that he loves her—as his wife with an exclusivity that no other woman on earth has a right to share. And she tells him that she loves him—as her husband, with the same uniqueness to which no other man on earth has a claim.

If even the least act of kindness is elevating and every token of charity makes us more God-like, what shall we say of the sanctifying power of the marital experience where, among Christians, it partakes of the sacrament they have received?

3. Sexual experience is sanctifying as restraint because in every marriage sometimes, and in some mar-

riages many times, the married couple must sublimate their natural desire for intercourse and express their mutual affection in other ways.

No two marriages are the same in this respect. But, given the normal differences between the sexes and the additional differences of mood, and temperament and state of health and attitude of mind—married people are to expect that each must often practice sexual self-restraint in a hundred different ways—if their love is to be promoted and not injured by marital intercourse. Whatever patience, prudence and forebearance this calls for is immensely sanctifying. After all, where there is true love between the spouses, they know it is fostered by mutual restraint and injured by selfish indulgence, no matter how the selfishness is popularly named.

4. Sexual experience is sanctifying as generosity because it is by their marital embrace that husband with wife generously welcome new human life into their lives according to the will of God. Their readiness to accept whatever children the Lord may wish to send them is more than avoiding sin. It is an expression of selfless altruism that puts into practice Christ's mandate of love sometimes to a heroic degree.

As the Savior made it plain throughout His public life, but especially at the Last Supper, love is always self-giving and self-effacing. Can anyone doubt that marital intercourse that is open to new life, in today's contraceptive world, is self-giving? Can anyone further doubt that such conjugal love is sanctifying? It is authentically Christian love because it is selfless love, with a selflessness that requires much grace and merits further grace from the God whose name is love.

Underlying this exalted concept of love is profession of faith in Christ's divinity. When He told His disciples to love others as He loved them, He was telling them to love their fellowman as He, Who is God, loves the world He created and then became man to redeem. God's love is boundless and totally generous. It is not coerced, but totally free. It is not self-seeking, but looks only to benefit the creatures whom God lovingly brought out of nothing to communicate to them, not yet existing, a share in His own infinitely happy being. The same God, with the same freedom and generosity, took on man's humanity —not to enrich Himself, since it meant suffering and the Cross—in order to give of His goodness and (as God) to receive no profit from man in return.

This is the kind of love that Christ, through His merits, enables the married faithful to practice not only between themselves but from themselves (as one flesh) toward the yet unknown and unconceived children whom Providence wants to entrust to their care.

The realism of this love is intelligible only where the faith on which it is based is strong and ready to give testimony to what it believes.

Hence the new-found role of matrimony as a sacrament of sanctification twice over: once to themselves, because God enriches with His blessings those who for love of Him love the children He wants to send them; and once again to other people who see such Christian witness of generosity in the midst of a sexually selfish and self-preoccupied world.

To such couples the Lord has entrusted the task of making visible to men the holiness and sweetness of the law which joins the mutual love of husband and wife to their cooperation with the love of God who is the Author of human life.

In this way, Christian husbands and wives help to sanctify the world by their witness in making visible to the world Christ's law of love by a two-fold visibility: by their marital fidelity, which testifies to their unitive love for each other; and by their marital generosity, which testifies to their procreative love of the children whom they bear.

Sex As Temperance

Our second level of reflection on the relationship between sex and sanctity is to see how sex as temperance is a means of growing in holiness.

Before we say anything more, however, it should be noted that God's creatures, here sex, can lead us to heaven and make us holy not only by being used but also by not being used. Everything that God made is good, because God made it; but its goodness for us depends on its being used in conformity with the will of God according to each one's state of life.

For those who are not married, or even though married in their relationship to anyone else than their own spouse, sex is sanctifying if it is not deliberately experienced. Another word for this is temperance.

We usually associate temperance with avoiding excess in food and especially drink. But actually temperance refers to the proper control of all our bodily and emotional impulses. When temperance refers to the control of the urge for sexual gratification it is called the moral virtue of chastity.

As such, it is morally binding on everybody, men, women and children; the married and the unmarried; priests, religious and the laity. All are bound by an obligation that is grave, to deliberately not indulge in sexual pleasure except in marriage, according to one's married state in life.

For the unmarried, therefore, the nature of chastity means total abstention from any deliberate desire for or indulgence of sexual (or, as we also call it, venereal) pleasure.

Hence, as the latest declaration of the Holy See makes clear, premarital relations are mortally sinful, so also are masturbation and homosexuality, and no amount of sentimentalism or psychologism can make these sins sinless.

Basically, then, sex as temperance is the virtue of chastity, but chastity as self-control. It means that through self-discipline and the help of God's grace a person refrains from deliberately giving in to a powerful human drive. The drive is powerful because on it finally depends the continuation of the human race. It has been compared with the instinct for self-preservation; only here it is the preservation of human society.

As such, sex as the virtue of temperance is knowable by reason and provable by human logic. If nothing else, we know that people who do not control their sex appetite end up not controlling other desires. They become victims of their lusts, and the hospitals and mental institutions have their share of the slaves of sex passion.

But one question still remains. How is sex as the virtue of temperance sanctifying? The answer is simple. Everything morally good we do in God's friendship is *ipso facto* sanctifying. We gain supernatural merit which means we grow in the divine life, every time we perform the least good action in the state of grace. And the degree of merit is proportionate, other things being equal, to the effort we put into whatever we do in the practice of virtue.

As everyone knows, the practice of self-control in sex demands more than ordinary effort. It has been called "The Difficult Commandment." Accordingly sex-control is not only pleasing to God but extraordinarily sanctifying.

Sex As Sacrifice

Our third and final reflection on sex as a means of sanctification goes beyond chastity as temperance. We may call it the practice of chastity as the love of God and the greater love of one's fellowman—but its essence is sacrifice.

Except for Christ's revelation on the subject, we should hardly know about the existence of this virtue, let alone would we see it put into practice.

What does this mean? It means that provided a person has the grace to make the sacrifice, he or she is able not only to restrain the sexual appetite but actually can offer up to God the pleasure to which we have a perfect natural right.

What are we saying? We are saying that, since the grace of Christ has been given to the human race, it is possible not only to practice sexual self-control but to make what we may call sexual self-sacrifice.

There is quite a difference between controlling, in the sense of not indulging, and surrendering, in the sense of freely and voluntarily giving up to God.

When I practice chastity as temperance, I am abstaining from a pleasure; and the abstention pleases God; and it makes me more holy because I am doing the will of God.

When I practice chastity as sacrifice, I am more than abstaining. I am willingly and (with divine grace) cheerfully offering God the pleasure as an oblation to the divine majesty. I am offering a sacrifice, which is the surrender of something precious, and sex is precious, out of love for God.

No other motive is adequate because no other will inspire a lifetime surrender of sexual experience except love. I elevate the virtue of temperance to a divine plane. I surrender what God and I know is a source of great and (in marriage) legitimate satisfaction not only because I fear to offend God but because I want to do something more for God by pleasing Him through this noble sacrifice.

But it is not only out of love of God that people undertake to practice consecrated chastity that we are calling sexual sacrifice. They are also moved by their love for others.

How so? We have the answer by now in the annals of human history since the time of Christ. Tens of thousands who wished to signalize themselves in the service of their neighbor, in the corporal and spiritual works of mercy, sacrificed the blessings of marriage. They knew what experience testifies, that loving chastity is really loving charity. It does many things:

—It liberates the human spirit to give itself generously to the service of others.

—It enlightens the human mind to see the needs of others and become extraordinarily thoughtful of their wants.

—It sensitizes the human heart to know human problems and want to relieve human misery.

And all the while, chastity as sexual sacrifice out of love sanctifies those who are faithful to their chaste commitment. It empowers them to draw close to the chaste Christ and His virgin Mother; and again, provided they are faithful to their generous surrender, it enables them to sanctify everyone who enters their lives and draw them nearer to God.

Epilogue

We began this conference by emphasizing the fact that Catholic Christianity considers the human body sacred. It was made by God as man's creator and was assumed by the Son of God in the Incarnation. I would like to close the conference by making this observation. It is unrealistic to even talk about sanctity, and impossible to achieve it unless a person takes sex seriously and sees it as a measure of his desire to please God.

Not all have the same calling and not all receive the same grace from the Almighty. But no believer in Christ can become holy unless the sexual desires in his or her life are in harmony with the will of God. Or, put it another way, everyone who loves God knows he must live a chaste life according to his vocation. Chastity in every state of life is the norm of a person's charity. Chaste people, whether married or single, whether priests, religious or the laity, are selfless people. They love God more than themselves and are therefore ready to prove their love always by self-control; if they are married, by the grateful use of their powers of generation according to the divine will; and if they are called to celibacy, by the generous surrender of an experience that divine revelation compares to the enjoyment of Paradise.

If we shall all finally be judged by our practice of charity, it is not too much to say we shall also be judged by our practice of chastity. Why? Because only the pure of heart shall see God; all others will be excluded from the marriage feast that God has prepared for those who love Him.

But chastity has its rewards already in this life, as anyone who sincerely tries to keep himself chaste can testify. It is not as though chastity were oppressive and sex indulgence exhilarating. Just the opposite. Chaste people are happy people; the unchaste are not happy. What a discovery for some people to make! That as they grow in self-mastery and use or sacrifice sex experience as God wants them to do, they grow in holiness, which is known to God alone. They also grow in happiness, which God wants us to have now as a foretaste of the heaven where "there will no longer be marriage or giving in marriage," and which is our destiny in the life to come.

CHAPTER FIVE

Morality and Sexuality: What the Church Teaches

Rev. William B. Smith, S.T.D.

At this time, in this lecture series and in our country, it is difficult to address questions of sexual morality without taking notice of a much publicized book; namely, *Human Sexuality: New Directions in American Catholic Thought.*[1]

This publication-event received varied mention in the secular press: *N.Y. Times* (7/7/77) favorable; *N.Y. Daily News* (6/8/77) unfavorable; while *Time* (6/13/77) and *Newsweek* (7/11/77) reported its challenge and reactions.

It is important to note that this study is not the work of the Catholic Theological Society of America as such, but rather, the work of a committee of five persons commissioned by that Society. Indeed, it was first other members of the C.T.S.A. who presented a collective critique of this book[2] which was followed by individual reviews of some length in most national Catholic weeklies. My own critique appeared in the *Register*.[3]

Post-publication reaction has been unusually large both in ecclesiastical circles (Doctrinal Committee of

N.C.C.B.[4]; individual bishops and dioceses) and in academic circles. No doubt this is because the largest part of the study (pp. 99-242) deals not with theoretical speculation but with "Pastoral Guidelines"—which is, of course, the proper province of the Pastors of the Church.

At this time it is fair to say that published scholarly reaction to the *Human Sexuality* study has been overwhelmingly negative.[5] Also, with the passage of time, further and fuller reviews have appeared which now serve more than one purpose. First, negative critiques continue, but thoughtful essays supportive of and explanatory of accepted Catholic teaching have appeared. Further, the May-Harvey collaboration, first published in *Communio*, has been expanded into booklet form in the Synthesis series of the Franciscan Herald Press.[6] This contains a nuanced critique of the committee's presuppositions and methodology which basics got them to the curious positions they espouse. This May-Harvey critique dismantles a current form of moral reasoning that extends far beyond the book in question.

Finally, there is a book in preparation that will be the fruit of twelve Catholic scholars (moral theologians; biblical scholars; and experts in Catholic doctrine and philosophy) which will be a welcome and reliable contribution to this field.

It is not my present purpose to critique that book at this time—nonetheless, the six points I will try to present, since they do support Catholic teaching, will also apply to the *Human Sexuality* study since the latter effort wanders far from Catholic teaching and often contradicts Catholic and even Christian morality.

1. Sexuality Is a Good

It is only conventional wisdom to speak of good and bad in actions as we speak of good and bad in things. Properly, it is only "human actions" that we describe as morally good, or, morally evil—actions done knowingly and from choice.

A first consideration of human sexuality is then to locate its place within the realm of morality and to do this without using adulterous or idolatrous terms. Human sexuality is a good. It is a God-created and therefore a God-given good. Sacred Scripture attests to this fact; so too does Sacred Tradition, both remote and recent (cf. SCDF, *Persona humana* [12/29/75] nos. 4; 5; 11; 12).[7]

Human sexuality is neither above nor beneath the realm of reason. Those who are fixed on its abuses seem to forget that there is a virtue of chastity; those who are fixed on its uses seem to forget that there can be abuses.

In our time and culture it is imperative to recall that there is a virtue of chastity and that chastity applies to everyone: single, married, celibate, widowed. Far too often—and for too many—chastity is taken to be a synonym for celibacy involving vows, whereas, of course, it is a Christian moral virtue and virtues are for all Christians. Just as the virtues are the key to Thomistic morality,[8] so too is the realization that chastity—as a virtue for all—is the key for locating human sexuality in the realm of Christian morality.

Human sexuality, in a Christian perspective, has at least two real dimensions, two goods and/or realities that must be served: at once, a life-giving good, and a love-giving good. When both of these inseparable realities are served and honored in act and in fact—in an ordered way—then this specific kind of human activity serves and honors its inherent values. Morally, this is called a good kind of activity. It is good because these constitutive dimensions of the human person are knowingly chosen and personally fulfilled.

Personal activity that acts against these goods—either the life-giving, or the love-giving, or both—is a wrong kind of activity since it renders asunder what God has joined together. Be it an individual instance or a pattern of incidents, these real constituents are separated and/or suppressed for some hoped for result that neither reason nor reality can guarantee.

We humans are no more pure persons than we are pure natures. Gnostics might prefer the former, materialists the latter and ancient or modern Dualists forever separate both. Many today prefer not to mention nature fearing perhaps that any reasoned consideration of nature is a throwback to the Middle Ages jeopardizing the "progress" of culture and history. Personalist insights are said to be opposed to and above bodily instincts. So pervasive is this dualism that every form of ethical situationism now in vogue is dualist to the core. Always, the control value, the master moral rubric is a subjective one—a personal good, a psychic good, an intentional good; but never a material bodily good.[9]

Authentic Christian tradition has been unwilling to separate and thus sacrifice either the life-giving (procreative) or the love-giving (unitive) dimension of human sexuality. Both are constitutive dimensions of human bodily existence. Christian chastity, then, is a virtue not for angels nor for animals but for human beings—persons who are bodies charged with intelligence and grace.

Catholic theology presents chastity as one of the essential elements of the virtue of temperance, the cardinal moral virtue that moderates human desires. In particular, chastity is that moral virtue which exercises reasonable control within the desires and pleasures of sex (*ST*, II-II, q.151,a.2).

One modern scholar describes it this way:[10]

"Chastity is one of the forms of the cardinal virtue of temperance and is concerned with integrating our sexual and affective loves and pleasures into our person, with the loving and intelligent ordering of our sexual desires and longings, of our need to touch and be touched. As an intelligent and loving ordering of our sexual loves, it is predicated on a truthful understanding of them and of the human purposes that they are given us to further."

Again, as above, we cannot tire of emphasizing that chastity is a moral virtue for everyone in every state in life. It is a needed and practiced perfection, not geared simply to avoiding faults, but aimed at attaining specific goods, connected goods and higher and other goods. Recent and ancient Catholic teaching locate this virtue properly; it is neither a narrow negation nor a restricted focus, rather:

> "It is a virtue which concerns the whole personality, as regards both interior and outward behavior. Individuals should be endowed with this virtue according to their state in life: for some it will mean virginity or celibacy consecrated to God, which is an eminent way of giving oneself more easily to God alone with an undivided heart. For others it will take the form determined by the moral law, according to whether they are married or single. But whatever the state of life, chastity is not simply an external state; it must make a person's heart pure in accordance with Christ's words: 'You have learned how it was said: You must not commit adultery. But I say this to you: if a man looks at a woman lustfully, he has already committed adultery with her in his heart'" (*Persona humana*, no. 11).

Legitimate pleasure is, of course, a good; but, just as obviously, it is not the only good. The history of ethical or moral theory reveals that entire systems of morality have been constructed with pleasure as *the* criterion of moral worth (cf. Hedonism; Epicureanism; Altruistic Hedonism).[11] Opposite to this, systems of Ethical Formalism have proposed a criterion of good and evil that so highlights a notion of "disinterested love" that even legitimate pleasure and satisfaction are not considered worthy components of virtue or even of good.[12] Catholic moral tradition has avoided both of these extremes. Rooted in Revelation, Catholic tradition has presented the doctrine of the virtues—first, theological; then, cardinal moral virtues, of which chastity is part and in which pleasure has its reasoned and reasonable place.

In explanation and in emphasis, Catholic moral tradition will avoid adulterous or idolatrous terms. That tradition sees and defends human sexuality as a good, an ordered good, open to and needing loving and intelligent direction. Indeed, the transformation of this reality into the realization of the good is a virtue—chastity.

2. The Pattern of Sexual Sins

Catholic moral tradition is a great respecter of realism. Insofar as anything has something real about it, it has something good about it. But, insofar as the real lacks something that should be there—like a real dimension; a constitutive dimension of human sexuality—it has something bad about it (ST,I-II, q.18,a.1).

Misleading and especially modern word usage can lead us away from reality. Several moral terms of reference have acquired such singular connotations that sex and sin are somehow seen to be coextensive. The terms "seduction" and "passion" very often now have a singular moral reference, when both terms have a broader and fuller comprehension.

The point here is not progressive or regressive semantics, the point is that unnuanced language might lead the speaker or the listener to think that the misuse of human sexuality is entirely in a class by itself. There are specific dimensions to be sure (cf. no. 3 below), but sin in this area is like sin in all areas—it is not unique of its kind.

Sin is first and fundamentally an offense against God.[13] Surely, Menninger was not the first to ask: whatever happened to sin? Much before, serious and actual theology asked the same basic question, Rondet being one author who put in faint form the foundational and prescient question posed by the late Pope Pius XII and repeated by his successors[14]—the great modern sin being to have lost the very sense of sin itself.

Apart from the slogan "it can't be wrong if it doesn't hurt anyone else" (see no. 6 below), the realism of ancient and recent Christianity requires that we recognize the disorder in which sexuality is very often exercised. Delhaye is correct in seeing "the disorder of sexual desire (as) a consequence of disobedience to God in fundamental guilt (i.e., original sin)," personal sins, lack of self-mastery and even contempt for the virtue of chastity.[15]

Above (no. 1) we spoke of the central and essentially related goods or realities of human sexuality in a Christian perspective (procreative and unitive). In every complete or incomplete action it is not necessary, or always possible, that both goods be realized in full, but it is never right to act directly against either. One way or another, separating or dissolving actions contradict the realities they are alleged to serve. The attempt objectively is to make (re-create; re-make) human sexuality other than what it is and what it is for. Metaphysically, this is an unreal try to fashion a reality of our own, and, morally it is not just dangerous but damaging. To manipulate God-given designs and purposes—for the best or worst motives —is to contradict the values these actions perfect and ensure.

Others have treated at length and perceptively what is at stake between the integrist and separatist advocates of human sexuality.[16] However fashionable or trendy, the separatist program and rationale is disordered and guarantees disorder. However camouflaged as "adult" or "progressive" or "enlightened," every disruption of God's order in creation—most often under the guise of human advancement—is a real echo of man's first arrogant failure to improve on divine Providence. The effort is to re-make or un-make reality not in the image and likeness of God, but in our own image and likeness, most often to our own liking.

The realities of love and life—as well as the transmission of both—require respect. The authentic use of human sexuality requires acts and patterns of actions that respect and foster both of these inseparably connected realities. Actions destructive of or contradictory to these basic values cannot honor the dignity of the person in whom these values can exist.

All Christians are called to holiness (*Lumen gentium*, 39-42) just as Christian virtues are for all Chris-

tians. To locate, and not dislocate, we must recall that
virtues are interdependent and interrelated. Alternative-
ly, there is no genus of personal sin unique in its kind. The
Scriptures themselves provide some famous "catalogues of
virtues and vices" which immediately became a basic
moral stance: the two ways (cf. *Didache; Epistle of Barnabas*).

We need only recall one such Pauline list to see that
misused sexuality was not the only sin and see as well that
St. Paul was emphatic about what did not lead to holiness:

> "...lewd conduct, impurity, licentiousness,
> idolatry, sorcery, hostilities, bickering, jealousy,
> outbursts of rage, selfish rivalries, dissensions, fac-
> tions, envy, drunkenness, orgies, and the like"
> (Gal. 5:19-21).

We are warned by the Apostle that those who do such
things will not inherit the kingdom. Clearly and obviously, no such action brings about the kingdom either.

In asking why is it that we do not do what the will
intends (Gal. 5:17; Rom. 7:15), the Apostle Paul does not
lead us into a dead-end of categorical no-noes, rather,
and characteristic of Christian Revelation, he speaks at
once of the nobility of the Christian calling and of grace
that saves and makes such effort possible:

> "In contrast, the fruit of the Spirit is love, joy,
> peace, patient endurance, kindness, generosity,
> faith, mildness and chastity. Against such there is
> no law. Those who belong to Christ Jesus have
> crucified their flesh with its passions and desires.
> Since we live by the Spirit, let us follow the Spirit's
> lead" (Gal. 5:22-25).

In a considerable study about "Pluralism and the
Unity of Theology," the *International Theological Commission* proposed a very useful rule for locating the thread
of Catholic unity amid numerous opinions. In morality,
we should first attend to genuinely theological sources:

"locating unchanging principles in Sacred Scripture, which are clarified by Sacred Tradition and presented in each age by the Magisterium" [17]

Both for sexual sins and their remedy, we should attend especially, but not exclusively, to the letters of the New Testament, their clarification in earliest and later Tradition, and a most recent magisterial declaration (*Persona humana*) whose final footnotes (nos. 27-43) provide an excellent and adequate source for securing the unity of Catholic teaching in this regard.

3. The Relative Importance of Sexual Morality

Some might ask, and others accuse, that the Church stresses sexual morality too much. Often enough, this is condensed in the accusation that the Church has a "hang-up" on sex. To determine who might be hung-up on what, one might consult the bestseller lists (fiction and non-fiction) of any popular book-review or weekend news supplement. The film, entertainment and advertising industries provide another societal indicator, none of which industries claim any special affinity with the Vatican. While the commercialization of sex is not solely an American phenomenon, its effect in our culture has been one of trivialization not enhancement.

Is sexual morality important? Yes, indeed it is; many personal and societal realities are involved, and that consideration cannot be stressed too much.

While the Church of tradition and the Church of today teaches that chastity is an important virtue, no orthodox teacher has or does maintain that it is the most important virtue. Both the catalogues of sins and the catalogues of virtues are long; sexual sins do not occupy the first place on that list nor are they morally the most deadly.

Nonetheless, as a specific part of the cardinal moral virtue of temperance there is an obvious foundation importance to temperance virtues. (Kindred realities are not seen as related in our society: abstinence and food, sobriety and drink. For a slim, trim figure no sacrifice or regimen is too much; unfortunately, drink in our culture is seen as a regimen in itself until, for too many, complete abstinence is the only path to sobriety.)

Virtues are interdependent and interrelated—higher and lower. Experience and the logic of many a Gospel parable teach that irresponsibility or incapacity at lower levels precludes higher ones. What is true of tasks and talents is true of virtue—especially the cardinal moral virtues.[18]

Further, there are essential human goods (realities) involved and at stake in human sexuality: the transmission of life, the transmission of love; interpersonal goods: friendship, fidelity, honesty and truth. Personal goods and goals are not the only consideration; marriage and family life are, by nature, social goods and intrinsic to the social fabric. These are not abstractions! What some present as allegedly "alternate and meaningful life-styles" are no mere style at all—they are an ideological assault on marriage and family life and are not part of a preparation for either.

In the recent moral pastoral of the U.S. Bishops (N.C.C.B., *To Live in Christ Jesus*, November 11, 1976), it is with good reason that the first section, "The Family," contains related and interrelated issues: the indissolubility of marriage (pp. 14-17); transmission of life—artificial birth control (pp. 17-19); the aged and euthanasia (pp. 20-22).[19]

The public, and many within the Church, has been slow to recognize and then realize how these questions—and the attitudes that foster them—interconnect. Viewing human sexuality in the covenant of marriage as the transmission of human life and the transmission of human love, when one attacks, denies or suppresses one of these co-essential ends the other purpose is essentially compromised.

Nuanced psychological and philosophical analyses are available for study,[20] but popular and public attitudes are already obvious and instructive. Acts that prevent and attitudes aimed at preventing "unwanted" babies *before* conception are consistent with acts and attitudes of disposing of "unwanted" babies *after* conception. Indeed, once you grant that being "unwanted" is a disease, then the same attitude is already in place to tolerate and accept such descriptions as "unwanted" parents, "unwanted" grandparents and "unwanted" commitments—with all that they imply.

Disordered practices and sad consequences on both a personal and societal level are not lacking. Personal scars, arrested growth, impaired development, no training, or worse, bad training, these are not cured by trendy slogans.[21] Collectively, social consequences multiply and the record of history is clear—no civilization of moment survived unregulated sexuality that either undermined or trivialized marriage and family life.

Curiously, some Marxist regimes[22] seem to perceive the natural connection and consequences of misused sexuality better than allegedly more developed nations. When a national news-weekly comments on the relatively low incidence of promiscuity or venereal disease in mainland China, the comments are patronizing—a puritan or prudish ethic lingers on. The inference and reference is perhaps that development and progress will come when such societies advance to if not equal our advanced levels of promiscuity and pandemic V.D.[23]

In the field of teaching and exposition, it is often charged that classic Catholic moral teaching—especially the moral manuals—were excessively concerned in content and minute detail with sexuality through an overkill emphasis in their presentation of the sixth and ninth commandments.

The publications of this past decade might reveal that a neat bit of transference is taking place here. No classic author approaches the percentage and concentration of some very current writers. Indeed, by actual line count, the accused do not stand guilty, rather it is the accusers who have a lopsided emphasis.

Father Charles Curran, writing on the present state of moral theology in view of what he considers healthy contradictory positions, singles out for special mention writers who:[24]

> "...frequently deny the existing teaching of the hierarchical magisterium on such issues as contraception, artificial insemination, masturbation and the generic gravity of sexual sins. Newer approaches have been taken to the question of homosexuality. Some Catholic theologians have argued against the moral norm condemning all sexual relationships outside marriage.... Contemporary theologians are calling for a re-thinking of the absolute prohibition against divorce...."

To be sure, this author mentions other denials and controversies, but his own published work and the bibliographies cited reveal a disproportionate concentration *de sexto* which is precisely the overemphasis some so cavalierly attribute to classic authors.

In fact, and by actual line count, the much maligned but now rarely studied manuals of moral theology are very measured in their treatments. The once widely used Noldin-Schmitt text is a three-volume work of some 2,050 numbers and 1,824 pages. Of this, 104 numbers of only 94 pages constitute the tract *"de Castitate."*[25] Another widely used textbook was M. Zalba's two-volume work of 2,458 pages. Here too, *"de Castitate"* accounts for only 115 pages.[26]

The classic, indeed the Common Doctor, St. Thomas Aquinas, is nothing less than the model of economy in his *ex professo* treatment of sexuality in his *Summa Theologiae*. Of the 512 questions in the *Summa* only a handful explicitly treat sexuality in II-II: chastity (q.151); virginity (q.152); the vice of lust in general (q.153); specific kinds of lust (q.154); continence (q.155); incontinence (q.156); and modesty (q.160).

Indeed, the telling contrast between the classic and most current works is the vast positive exposition of connected and interconnected virtues which so dominates the *Summa* and is so obviously absent from most recent efforts. Apart from current content being disproportionately questions of sexuality, a further disproportionate emphasis seems to be theories of compromise and/or justifying the lesser evil which, perhaps lesser, still remains evil. In point of fact, most methodological or theoretical speculations—often called "revisions"—seem bent on justifying for our age what no previous age ever considered Christian behavior; and this is especially so in the use and abuse of human sexuality.

4. Gravity of Sexual Sins

The generic gravity of sexual sins is often said to be unique in that every deliberate sexual gratification outside of well-ordered conjugal love is grave matter when directly intended. The classic reference is to sins of impurity—completed, incipient or internal—in which there is no slightness of matter *(parvitas materiae)*.

The statement refers to impurity (where sexual pleasure is involved) not to immodesty. It is not correct to say that there can be no venial sin against the sixth commandment; it is correct to say that there can be no fully deliberate sin of impurity which does not involve grave matter.

True, failures of malice are worse than those of weakness; and sins of the mind differ from those of the body. But, the principle at stake, properly defined, is not unique to sexual sins. Formal blasphemy and perjury, directly intended, do not admit of parvity of matter, nor would formal tempting of God and some kinds of simony of divine law. Also, there are no circumstances in which the deliberate denial of the Faith could be anything except grave matter.[27]

What particular basis is there for this conventional teaching? First, the Scriptures themselves leave no doubt about the generic gravity of sexual sins: cf. Eph. 5:5; Gal. 5:19-21; Col. 3:5; for internal/mental, Mt. 5:28. These and similar texts should be read and studied, not merely cited. The Fathers and Doctors of Catholic Tradition have consistently maintained what is within the scope of these biblical norms as has the Magisterium, most recently in *Persona humana:*

> "Now according to Christian tradition and the Church's teaching, and as right reason also recognizes, the moral order of sexuality involves such high values of human life that every direct violation of this order is objectively serious" (*PH*, no. 10).

The documentation offered for this citation is itself instructive (cf. *PH*, no. 10, ftnt. 24) in that the Congregation for the Doctrine of the Faith refers to a condemned moral thesis of the 17th century and to two sections of the encyclical *Humanae vitae* (nos. 13-14). The full reference includes a long and consistent magisterial teaching on premarital chastity and masturbation.[28]

The conventional authors support the same doctrine. Häring, for example, writing in his orthodox phase says:[29]

> "The thesis as we give it here with all its apparent rigor merely means that all acts in their end and meaning, which involve a fundamental selfishness in the sexual life—whether satisfaction be complete or incomplete—constitute a serious disorder and are calculated to jeopardize man in his moral integrity. They are grave sins."

Again, as above, this consideration is apart from the covenant of marriage, and the focus is objective or intrinsic morality. Most often the designation of mortal or venial refers to sin which is properly a subjective category understood in terms of fault, blame or culpability. The Declaration, *Persona humana,* consistently and correctly carries through the objective/subjective distinction in nuanced and precise moral terms.

Each mention carefully includes the concept of finality and the objective (intrinsic) referent:

> (general):
> "...the finality of the sexual act *(de actus sexualis finalitate)* and on the principal criterion of its

morality: it is respect for its finality that ensures the moral goodness of this act..." *(PH*, no. 5).

.   (pre-marital):

"...love must find its safeguard in the stability of marriage, if sexual intercourse is truly to respond to the requirements of its own finality *(finalitatis sibi propriae)* and to those of human dignity..." *(PH*, no. 7).

(homosexuality):

"...For according to the objective moral order, homosexual relations are acts which lack an essential and indispensable finality.... Homosexual acts are intrinsically disordered *(intrinseca natura esse inordinatos)* and can in no way be approved" *(PH*, no. 8).

(masturbation):

"...masturbation is an intrinsically and seriously disordered act *(esse actum intrinsice graviterque inordinatum)*.... The deliberate use of the sexual faculty outside normal conjugal relations essentially contradicts the finality of the faculty *(essentialiter eius fini contradicit)*" *(PH*, no. 9).

And thus, in no. 10—"...every direct violation of this (moral) order is objectively serious *(ordinis obiective sit gravis) (PH*, no. 10).

It should be helpful to delineate, as the Declaration does, objective morality in the context of the finality of sexual acts, the moral import of which is clearly circumscribed within the finality of marriage. This foundation covenant has a proper and created finality, since, as Vatican II teaches, it "has been established by God and qualified by His laws." For the good of the spouses and offspring and society there exists a sacred bond that "no longer depends on human decisions alone" *(GS*, no. 48). It is, then, in continuity with the teaching of the Council that *Persona humana* highlights high values of human life in this statement:

"Now according to Christian tradition and the Church's teaching, and as right reason also recog-

nizes, the moral order of sexuality involves such
high values of human life that every direct violation
of this order is objectively serious" (*PH*, no. 10).

Thus, the encyclical *Humanae vitae* (nos. 13 and 14) is
cited as a recent reaffirmation that in fidelity to God's
design the transmission of life and the transmission of love
involve not simply a personal good but the good of the
human race as well.

In truth, this line of reasoning is more in accord with
the older and wider moral teaching of St. Thomas rather
than the later more juridic classification according to
commandments (cf. *ST*,I-II,q.88,a.2). The whole second
part of the *Summa* is the progress of the creature toward
his God. Thus, as the more astute commentators point
out, the casuist will place the mortality of mortal sin on
the gravity of the precept violated, whereas, for St. Thomas the mortality of mortal sin is its opposition to charity.
"The progress of the human spirit toward the enjoyment
of the good which is God is the act proper to charity."[30]

At the same time, this consideration of the generic
gravity of deliberate sexual sins, outside the covenant of
marriage, is not without prudential judgment arising, as
Häring writes, from "an experience and understanding of
the human soul." [31] It is precisely because of the natural
intensity of sexual passions that they have "a great power
of anarchy and destruction of the person." It is because of
the anarchic tendency that Ple writes the desires of the
flesh strongly resist integration.[32] The same author
perceptively describes the disintegration of connected
virtues and values when human sexuality is misused, as
for example, hope, fear, despair, audacity, anger, abstinence, sobriety, humility, prudence, fortitude, justice
and the virtue of religion.[33]

Finally, the approved authors present some nuanced
distinctions regarding intrinsic evil which are not always
appreciated. For them, there are kinds of acts considered
in se evil or absolutely so, and, those seen as *per se* evil—
intrinsically wrong because of some conjoined condition,
attendant circumstance or some danger very much con-

nected with the action.[34] It does not take much pastoral experience to realize the attendant, actual and factual dangers to the life of charity in us that are so much connected, indeed, intrinsic to deliberately willed sexual disorder. Yet, appreciating the connected and attendant dangers is all that much more difficult for those who fail to realize that deliberately placing ourselves in a proximate occasion of sin is itself sinful.

Let us conclude this point as we began, rooted in Revelation. We Catholic Christians look for the resurrection of the dead and the life of the world to come. We look and live for salvation—for salvation of body and soul. Not just the salvation of the soul, but for resurrected life of the whole person, body and soul.

To live in Christ means that real life is hidden now with Christ in God (Col. 3:1-4). In the covenant of marriage, there is a two-in-one flesh: a great foreshadowing, that refers to Christ and the Church (Eph. 5:31-32).

Outside the covenant of marriage, we who are bodies are so for the Lord (1 Cor. 6:13). We are temples of the Holy Spirit (1 Cor. 6:19), members of Christ (1 Cor. 6:15), to profane that temple, to prostitute that member contradicts the life of Christ in us. St. Paul reminds us that other sins are outside the body (1 Cor. 6:15) but the fornicator sins against his own body which is the Lord's. "You are not your own. You have been purchased, and at a price. So glorify God in your body" (1 Cor. 6:19-20; also Rom. 6:19-23). Gnostics we are not! Thus, we offer God worship and adoration in spirit and in truth which our bodies owe Him. Indeed, rooted in Revelation and Tradition, the Church continues to teach that very high virtues and values are at stake here.

5. Slogans That Don't Help

Apart from the biblical dead-end of making a positive mystique out of sin, some explicit and implicit appeals for more and more experience should be rejected decisively. Large amounts of undigested self-realization jargon have been swallowed by the most unsuspecting minds. Slogans abound, but wisdom and virtue do not. Some, for example, would have it that "bad sex is better than no sex."

Apart from defying simple logic, this cheap pearl of no price is not much removed from the many experience-laden slogans wherein vice becomes virtue and vice versa. Are we to believe that bad politics is better than no politics; indeed, that bad cover-ups are better than no cover-ups; and that bad Watergates are better than no Watergates? It is not at all clear how or if or even why such are presented as alternatives.

Nonetheless, there is a persistent thread, in careless moral slogans, that provided you are "open," "explicit" or especially "blatant" about something, then that something curiously becomes a virtue because you are "open" about it. Of course, "open" murder at high-noon on Main Street morally remains murder. The fact that one is very "open" about it does not and cannot change the moral species of murder—it is and remains a bad kind of act.

In the rush to come out of the closet, many wrong kinds of moral acts have been invested with a bogus kind of dignity simply because one is open and/or blatant about them. Oscar Wilde was closer to the truth in commenting that hypocrisy is not all that bad—after all, it's the tribute vice pays to virtue.

The connection and interconnection between morality and social sciences is a nuanced one, but it is not a simple equation.[35] Moral research welcomes the sound findings of both psychological and sociological research; just as moralists also welcome "heavies" in respective fields doing a better job of exposing and/or disposing of "lightweights" in the same field.

Norman Mailer has pointed out that many are guilty of "skimming"—i.e., skimming off the jargon and expression of a science without really studying that science. This has, of course, the neat advantage of improving our vocabularies without ever disturbing our point of view.

Thus, Philippe Delhaye registers his disapproval of a certain tendency among some sociologists—the "masters of suspicion," he calls them—who do not so much question objectivity as consider objectivity as out of the question entirely.

Some no longer seek the truth or the facts but simply record personal reactions. Obviously, sociological research is very useful if one wishes to know states of minds. But, this becomes dangerous when such "findings" replace doctrinal or critical judgment. There begins, what Delhaye calls, a certain "hypertrophy of the ego" which does not esteem the truth or the facts so much as it fosters an exaggerated pluralism, implying largely that there is no objective morality worth investigating but the only effort worthy of investigation is the different ways different people look at and value different things. Thus would morality become simply another chapter in a sociology book.[36]

Another area of unflective overemphasis—with profound impact on moral practice—is that of "psychobabble." By this, I mean no criticism of sound psychology; but rather, those forms and expressions of pop psychology, especially the much celebrated "fluid and uncommitted self" that renders a Christian commitment to Christian virtues meaningless, if not perverse.

Of late, psychologists and psychiatrists of some standing have challenged some of the more fashionable exponents of pop psychology. The book of William K. Kilpatrick[37] is a much welcomed corrective for the flights of Norman O. Brown, Alvin Toffler and the Human Potential Movement in general, which functions, in particular, as a masquerade of escapism.

R. D. Rosen has coined the term "Psychobabble"[38] which he outlines as the fast-talk and quick-cure in the "era of feeling." He subjects to critical review: W. Erhard's "EST," L. Orr's "Rebirthing," A. Janov's "Primal Therapy," E. Berne's "Transactional Analysis," D. Viscott's "Self-Help Phenomenon" and finds them lacking. In effect, most of the jargon ("psychobabble") proclaims: "you're all right baby!" which does no more than mask real problems, abdicate responsibility, promote narcissism and does nothing for real psychological problems except postpone and compound them. It is for these reasons that I say slogans don't help.

6. It Can't Be Wrong If It Doesn't Hurt Someone Else!

The consequentialist calculus of what doesn't-hurt-anybody-else has come into its own of late. However, as a moral theory it is inadequate in what it presupposes and in what it overlooks.

Intrinsic to the it-doesn't-hurt-anyone-else rubric is a distorted notion of rights and abilities. Often, one hears the remark: I have a perfect right to do what I want with my own body! This is not a statement of one who lives *in* and *for* the Lord. Rather, it is the presupposition of the self-created humanist who really believes in his or her own absolute moral autonomy.

Apart from confusing the *moral right* to do something with the *physical ability* to do something, the advocates of absolute moral autonomy simply do not realize or will not acknowledge the true source and goal of human life. Years ago, C. S. Lewis pinpointed this shortcoming in outlining "The Three Parts of Morality." Many do understand and do acknowledge that they must not destroy or damage others, but they honestly think that what they do with what they think is their own—that is their own business entirely:[39]

> "But does it not make a great difference whether I am, so to speak, the landlord of my own mind and body, or only a tenant, responsible to the real landlord? If somebody else made me, for his own purposes, then I shall have a lot of duties which I should not have if I simply belong to myself....
>
> "It seems then that if we are to think about morality, we must think of all three departments:

relations between man and man; things inside each man; and relations between man and the power that made him. We can all cooperate in the first one. Disagreements begin with the second and become serious with the third. It is in dealing with the third that the main differences between Christian and non-Christian morality come out."

The consequentialist posture that it can't be wrong if it doesn't hurt someone else—a notion central to situationism—has affected not only apparently private decisions (suicide and assisted suicide) but has flowed over and into euthanasia, abortion and rapid divorce all of which have clear societal consequences.

In a parallel fashion, misplaced moral sovereignty has escalated a mistaken notion of the alleged "rights" of conscience. In this regard, even traditional moralists have, at times, overworked the concept of subjective imputability to the detriment of objective morality.

To be sure, the proper distinctions between correct/erroneous and certain/doubtful conscience remain. With a certain but erroneous conscience there may be no fault but that does not mean that there is no problem. Frank Sheed points out in a recent book that the laws of morality are, at least, laws: honesty, purity, fidelity to promised word. They are as much laws as are the laws of diet, and defective conduct damages us as much as defective diet does.[40]

The prevailing notion of no-fault morality may be comforting on the surface, but, if pursued, it is quite misleading. True, if you mistakenly take poison, there is no moral fault; but that mistaken person is going to be sick, maybe even die.

No-fault insurance may cover financial loss, but the car trunk if dented must be fixed. No-fault divorce may disperse moral blame, but that marriage is now painfully broken. With little fault, or even no fault at all, one cannot keep doing what is objectively wrong without real damage.

It is a false and misleading delusion to entertain the moral thesis that significant human relations—and human sexuality is at least that—can be hermetically sealed off in slogans of moral autonomy without personal or social consequences. Indeed, significant societal consequences are the very consequence of the consequentialist ethic. In the concrete, there is no such thing as a moral vacuum. And in the absence of a recognizable virtue of chastity, one finds and even expects the presence of vice in so many personal and societal trends.

As we began, let us conclude. Even when the right thing is done, the "how" and "why" of the good done matters greatly. Right actions done for the right reasons build that internal quality, that character called "virtue," [41] and it is the virtue of chastity that most needs to be fashioned, fostered and practiced by us in private and in public. The saints speak of this with clarity and truth:

> "Be imitators of God as his dear children. Follow the way of love, even as Christ loved you. He gave himself for us as an offering to God, a gift of pleasing fragrance.
> "As for lewd conduct or promiscuousness or lust of any sort, let them not even be mentioned among you; your holiness forbids this. Nor should there be any obscene, silly, or suggestive talk; all that is out of place. Instead, give thanks. Make no mistake about this: no fornicator, no unclean or lustful person—in effect an idolater—has any inheritance in the kingdom of Christ and of God. Let no one deceive you with worthless arguments. These are sins that bring God's wrath down on the disobedient; therefore have nothing to do with them" (Eph. 5:1-7).

Notes

1. A. Kosnik, *et all*, *Human Sexuality: New Directions in American Catholic Thought* (N.Y.: Paulist Press, 1977), 322 pages.

2. W. May; R. Lawler; J. Harvey; W. Smith; H. Sattler; E. Carroll; G. Kelly, in *National Catholic Register*, v. 8 (6/5/77), p. 8.

3. Cf. *National Catholic Register*, v. 8 (6/19/77), pp. 6-7; (6/26/77), 7-8; (7/3/77), p. 8.

4. Committee on Doctrine, N.C.C.B., "Statement Concerning: Human Sexuality" (Nov. 15, 1977), in *Origins*, v. 7, no. 24 (12/1/77), 376-378; (available from Publications Office of USCC, Wash., D.C.; order number B-126).

5. W. May in *Linacre Quarterly* 44 (Aug. 1977), 278-280; R. McInerny in *Commonweal* 104 (8/5/77), 505-507; W. May-J. Harvey in *Communio* 4 (Fall, 1977), 195-225; F. Meehan in *America* 137 (10/15/77), 230-234; G. Montague in *America* 137 (10/29/77), 284-285; G. Coleman in *The Priest* 33 (Nov. 1977), 12-15; 19-21; J. Casey in *Homiletic & Pastoral Review* 78 (Dec. 1977), 18-28; J. Connery in *Theological Studies* 39 (June 1978), 366-368.

6. W. E. May-J. F. Harvey, "On Understanding *Human Sexuality*" (synthesis series) (Chicago: Franciscan Herald Press, 1977), 79 pages.

7. Sacred Congregation for the Doctrine of the Faith, *Persona Humana* (Dec. 29, 1975), in *AAS* 68 (1976) 77-96 (hereafter *PH*). For a combined translation, I, "Declaration On Certain Questions Concerning Sexual Ethics," and, II, Commentaries, confer: publication (V-518) of same title (Wash., D.C.: USCC, 1977), 165 pages. (Contributors: C. Caffara; Ph. Delhaye; S. Garofalo; R. Spiazzi; J. Lejeune; G. Carriquiry; P. Sardi; D. Capone; M. Benzo; B. Ahern; H.C. Volk; R. Spiazzi-J. Visser.)

8. V.J. Bourke, *The History of Ethics* (N.Y.: Doubleday, 1968), pp. 98-99.

9. G. Grisez, "Dualism and the New Morality," Atti Del Congresso Internazionale Thommaso D'Aquino (1974) in *L'Agir Morale*, vol. 5 (Naples: Ed. Dominicane Italiane, 1977), pp. 323-330.

10. W.E. May, *The Nature and Meaning of Chastity* (synthesis series) (Chicago: Franciscan Herald Press, 1976), p. 36.

11. For Hedonism cf. *New Catholic Encyclopedia* 6:983-4; re Epicureanism cf. *NCE* 5:466-468; re Altruistic Hedonism, *NCE* 14:503-504. Also cf. V.J. Bourke, *op. cit.*, ch. 3 and 10.

12. For Ethical Formalism" cf. *NCE* 5:570. Also, T. Gilby (ed. trns.) *Summa Theologiae* (vol. 16) (N.Y.: McGraw-Hill, 1969), pp. 144-150.

13. For "sin" cf. *NCE* 13:236-245; Vatican Council II, *SC.*, no. 109; *LG.*, no. 11; *Ordo Paenitentiae* (Dec. 2, 1973), "Praenotanda," no. 5.

14. H. Rondet, *The Theology of Sin* (ND. Ind.: Fides, 1960). P. Pius XII (To Lenten Preachers, Feb. 23, 1944) in *AAS* 36 (1944), pp. 69-87. P. Paul VI (March 25, 1970) in *The Teachings of Paul VI—1970*, 3 (Wash., D.C.: USCC, 1971), 94-98, at 96.

15. Ph. Delhaye, in SCDF, *I, Declaration, II, Commentaries, op. cit.*, p. 52.

16. G. Grisez, *op. cit.*; W.E. May, *Sex, Love and Procreation* (synthesis series) (Chicago: Franciscan Herald Press, 1976), 53 pages (original in *HPR* 76, May, 1976, pp. 10ff.).

17. *La Documentation Catholique*, v. 70, no. 1632 (May 20, 1973), p. 460; trans. in London *Tablet* 227 (7/7/73), p. 647.

18. A. Ple, *Chastity and the Affective Life* (N.Y.: Herder and Herder, 1966), pp. 138-143.

19. N.C.C.B., *To Live in Christ Jesus* (11/11/76) (Wash., D.C.: Pub. Off. USCC, B-115, 1976), 48 pages; pp. 14-22.

20. G. Grisez, "Natural Family Planning Is Not Contraception," *Intnl. Rev. Natural Family Planning*, v. 1, no. 2 (Summer 1977), 121-126.

21. A. Ple, *ibid*. Ple explains that the temperate person realizes the integration of his person and not its mutilation. His effort sheds helpful light on what psychologists call the dissociated being, pp. 127-131. He also provides a full chapter on the spiritual, psychological and practical principles that make for an "Education to Chastity," pp. 150-171.

22. For a Marxist defense of family and family life, together with a severe critique of "Open Marriage" and non-binding commitments, confer: C. Lasch, *Haven in a Heartless World: The Family Besieged* (N.Y.: Basic Books, 1977).

23. Cf. *Newsweek* cover story on China (Sept. 1975); also see *Newsweek* 79 (7/19/72), 34-5; 87 (4/19/76), 38-40; 88 (9/4/76), 30-34.

24. C.E. Curran, "Moral Theology: The Present State of the Discipline," *Theological Studies* 34 (1973), p. 456.

25. Noldin-Schmitt-Heinzel, *Summa Theologiae Moralis*, 3 vols. (ed. 33) (Innsbruck: Felizian Rauch, 1960).

26. M. Zalba, *Theologiae Moralis Compendium*, 2 vols. (Madrid: B.A.C., 1958).

27. Confer: Council of Trent, *DS*. 1536-1537; Vatican Council I, *DS*. 3014; 3036.

28. SCDF, *Persona humana*, no. 10, ftnt. 24 citing ftnt. 17 for *DS*. 835; *DS*. 1367; *DS*. 2045; *DS*. 2148. Ftnt. 19, *DS*. 687-8; *DS*. 2149; and Allocutions of P. Pius XII (Oct. 8, 1953 and May 19, 1956).

29. B. Häring, *The Law of Christ*, vol. 3 (Westminster, Md.: Newman Press, 1966), pp. 291-296, at 291. Also cf. Noldin-Schmitt-Heinzel, *op. cit.*, I, "de Castitate," no. 11, 2, pp. 17-18; M. Zalba, *op. cit.*, I, nos. 1380-1381, pp. 750-3; Aertnys-Damen-Visser, *Theologia Moralis*, vol. 2 (ed. 18) (Rome: Marietti, 1968), no. 195, I, pp. 175-177.

30. T.C. O'Brien (tns.) *Summa Theologiae* (vol. 27) (N.Y.: McGraw-Hill, 1974): I-II, q. 88, a.2, ftnt. "k," pp. 52-3. Also, Ple, *op. cit.*, pp. 172-184.

31. B. Häring, *op. cit.*, 3:292.

32. Ple, *op. cit.*, p. 135.

33. *Ibid.*, pp. 138-143.

34. Aertnys-Damen-Visser, I, no. 59, II, pp. 88-89; Noldin-Schmitt-Heinzel, I, no. 71, 3°, p. 73; M. Zalba, I, no. 239, 3°, p. 129; and, no. 322, 1°, p. 188.

35. Cf. J.M. Gustafson, "What Is Normatively Human?" in his *Theology and Christian Ethics* (Phila.: Pilgrim Press, 1974), pp. 229-244.

36. P. Delhaye, "Reflection on the Problem of Pluralism in the Church," in *Problems of the Church Today* (Wash., D.C.: Pub. Off. USCC, V-415, 1976), pp. 31-46, at 38.

37. W.K. Kilpatrick, *Identity and Intimacy* (N.Y.: Dell, 1975).

38. R.D. Rosen, *Psychobabble* (N.Y.: Atheneum, 1977).

39. C.S. Lewis, *Mere Christianity* (ed. 17, paper) (N.Y.: Macmillan Paperbacks, 1973), p. 73.

40. F. Sheed, *The Church and I* (N.Y.: Doubleday, 1974), p. 311.

41. C.S. Lewis, *op. cit.*, p. 77.

CHAPTER SIX

Catechesis and Sexuality:
What the Church Teaches

Msgr. Eugene Kevane

This topic raises a question whether the Church has a position in catechetics, and if so, whether it touches the field of human sexuality? There is the attendant question whether the publication commissioned by the Catholic Theological Society of America violates this position in catechetics, and if so, just how—whether dangerously and grievously, or whether perhaps lightly in a way to be overlooked in practice.[1]

In answering the question whether the Catholic Church has a position in catechetics, there are larger perspectives to consider than the immediate documents of the living magisterium in the decades of recent time. For the Catholic Church has been teaching the Word of God faithfully during all the centuries since the apostles. In this teaching, the Catholic Church has continued from the Hebrews of the Old Law a manner of forming children and young people to a way of life by using the teaching device of "The Two Ways": the Way of Life on the one hand and the contrasting, diametrically opposed Way of Death, on the other. These larger perspectives bring us to the field of catechetics as such, the process of handing on the Word of God by teaching. For catechesis is the ministry of the Word, the revealed Word of God, a ministry to the very Word of God Incarnate.[2]

This Word of God to mankind across all earthly time is one and the same in all cultures and in all developments of culture. This Word of God constitutes the moral order by telling man two fundamental truths. First, there are two ways, the Way of Life and the Way of Death. Secondly, man is created free to choose one or the other.

I
The Way of Life

It was the very essence of Moses' prophetic mission to confirm his people in the knowledge of their own physical origin in Abraham because of a special divine purpose, a matter which gives insight into the revealed Word of God to which catechesis ministers. In the generations since the beginning and during the long dispersion of men in various tongues over the earth, a deep moral decline had set in. By Abraham's time it was far advanced. At this point God called Abraham as prophets were called, called him to come out from among this corrupted and depraved humanity, called him to become the progenitor of a new People of God for the salvation of all mankind. Clearly this was to be a people of the prophetic light, living on a new and higher level of relationship to the Supreme Being, illuminated by divine truth coming from above. Such was always the self-understanding of the Hebrews. "Now the Lord said to Abraham: 'Get out of your country and from your kindred and from your father's house, onto the land that I will show you and I will make of you a great nation, and I will bless you...so Abram went, as the Lord had spoken unto him..." (Gen. 12:1-4).

By responding in faith to this Word from on high, Abraham became the father of all who thus believe. As the Scriptures convey over and over, Abraham and all the prophets and all the people whom they formed placed their faith in this God as the Creator of the universe and hence as the master of its laws. Yahweh is a personal

God, the Father Almighty, Creator of heaven and earth, Creator of nature and human nature, Creator and Ruler of the laws of nature and human nature, the One who calls men to truly human dignity and immortal destiny.

Abraham is the man of faith in this Word of God which he understood by the prophetic light. He responded by faith to the call to leave the morally corrupted Gentile world of Ur of the Chaldees. Faith sustained him in the sacrifice of Isaac, his cherished only son who depended for existence upon the direct intervention of the Almighty and whom he would have sacrificed in obedience to the Word of this same God.

From Abraham, Moses' people had come forth, a nation of the prophetic light, who had issued as a people from Abraham, Isaac and Jacob, prophets of Yahweh. Faith in the Word of God was therefore to characterize this people. Their entire national life centered upon hearing this revealed word, practicing it as their religious way of life, and bearing it forward in history by teaching it to their children. "Men do not believe," Daniélou writes, "if they think in a general way that God exists, but do not for one moment think that God takes any part in history."[3] Taught by Moses and all the prophets, the Hebrews believed in God as a transcendent reality distinct from this visible cosmos. He is the Father Almighty, the One whose Providence reaches to the details of human life, the One who is man's ever-present helper, the One who is to be called upon in prayer. This is *Yahweh*, the God of the Hebrews, the Creator and hence the Lord and Lawgiver of creation.

Parallel with this elevated concept of God, the Word of God teaches a wonderfully lucid insight into man's nature, his weakness, his greatness, his calling from God. Man is the creature of God; his first obligation is to recognize his creaturehood. Man is a moral being, created by God with the dignity and challenge of freedom regarding the law of his Maker. At the same time, as the Hebrews knew both from experience and from the prophetic teaching, this creature lives in an actual condition which is prone to sinful disregard of his Creator, to the wrong use of this precious gift of moral freedom.

The Hebrew Revelation, then, the Word of God to which catechesis ministers, can be considered from the practical or catechetical point of view as a teaching and formation unto the way of life which the prophets gave to the Hebrews in the name of God. From Abraham's call away from the pagan corruptions, it is the way of life that contrasts with the pagan way of death.

In programmatic fashion the Book of Psalms opens with the contrast between these two ways as its theme.

"Happy is the man that has not walked in the council of the wicked, nor stood in the way of sinners...but his delight is in the Law of the Lord; and in his Law does he meditate day and night. And he shall be like a tree planted by streams of water, that brings forth its fruit in its season.... Not so, not so the wicked; but they are like the chaff which the wind drives away. Therefore the wicked shall not stand in the judgment nor sinners in the congregation of the righteous. For the Lord regards the way of the righteous; but the way of the wicked shall perish" (Psalm 1).[4]

This Hebrew religion, the unique religion of the revealed Word of God, is a way of life—better, it is *the* Way of Life. It is the way of the immortal human spirit that knows Yahweh and moves toward Him as the happy destiny of the blessed. The basic article of the Hebrew faith, the *Shema* which Moses received with God's commandments, binds the Israelite to Yahweh in a personal way of faith that unites the prophetic doctrine with human living. This constitutes the Way of Life. "Hear, O Israel, the Lord our God, the Lord is One. And you shall love the Lord your God with all your heart, and with all your soul, and with all your might. And these words which I command you this day shall be upon your heart; and you shall teach them diligently unto your children, and shall talk of them when you sit in your house and when you walk by the way and when you lie down and when you rise up. You shall bind them for a sign upon your hand, and they shall be frontlets between your eyes and you shall write them upon doorposts of your house and upon your gates" (Dt. 6:4-9).

"And God spoke all these words, saying: I am the Lord your God.... You shall have no other gods before me...you shall not take the name of the Lord your God in vain.... Remember the sabbath day, to keep it holy.... Honor your father and your mother.... You shall not murder. You shall not commit adultery. You shall not steal.... You shall not covet your neighbor's house...[nor] your neighbor's wife.... You yourselves have seen that I have talked with you from heaven" (Ex. 20:1-19).

This doctrine of the two ways, the two contrasting choices open before man's freedom, is the common theme of biblical revelation. This is its practical aspect, which constitutes the field of catechetics as a teaching that forms unto the Way of Life. Let us hear a few passages of the Scriptures which document this fact that there is a Way of Life contrasting with another way, the Way of Death.

"See, I have set before you this day life and good, death and evil, in that I command you this day to love the Lord your God, to walk in his ways, and to keep his commandments and his statutes and his ordinances; then you shall live and multiply and the Lord your God shall bless you in the land whither you go to possess it. But if your heart turn away and you...worship other gods and serve them; I declare unto you this day that you shall surely perish; you shall not prolong your days upon the land, whither you pass over the Jordan to go in to possess it. I call heaven and earth to witness against you this day, that I have set before you life and death, the blessing and the curse; therefore, choose life, that you may live, you and your seed; to love the Lord your God, to hearken to his voice; and to cleave to him, for that is your life and the length of days, that you may dwell in the land which the Lord swore to your fathers, to Abraham, to Isaac, to Jacob, to give them. And Moses went and spoke these words to all Israel" (Dt. 30:15-20; 31, 1).

The catechetical dimension of practical religious teaching involved in this way of life is stated over and over in the Bible, for it was the very substance of the national life of the Hebrews and indeed remains so to this day. Moses demands a teaching program for the Word of God: "But as for you, stand here by me and I will speak to you all the commandments and statutes and ordinances which you shall teach them, that they may do them in the land which I give them to possess. You shall observe therefore to do as the Lord your God has commanded you; you shall not turn aside to the right hand or to the left. You shall walk in all the way in which the Lord your God has commanded you that you may live so that it may be well with you that you may prolong the days you shall possess. Now this is the commandment, the statutes and the ordinances which the Lord your God commanded to teach you, that you might do them in the land...that you might fear the Lord your God to keep all his statutes and commandments, which I command you, you and your son, and your son's son, all the days of your life; and that your name may be prolonged. Hear, therefore, O Israel and observe to do it, that it may be well with you and that you may increase mightily, as the Lord, the God of your fathers, has promised unto you, a land flowing with milk and honey" (Dt. 5:31—6:3).

The two ways are set before the free choice of the people of God, as a blessing and a curse. "Behold, I set before you this day a blessing and a curse: the blessing, if you shall hearken unto the commandments of the Lord your God which I command you this day; and the curse, if you shall not hearken under the commandments of your Lord and God but turn aside out of the way which I command you this day, to go after other gods, which you have not known" (Dt. 11:26-28).

In the Book of Genesis, this path traced by divine revelation is called "the way of the Lord, to do righteousness and justice" (Gen. 18:19). This is the way to which God called Abraham, the father of a new people of God following this way of justice and holiness.

The prophets of Israel saw as their basic mission the confirmation of the people of God in this way of revealed truth and justice, recalling them to its path when they strayed. Let Jeremiah stand as an example of the tone and content of the prophetic teaching across the centuries. "And onto this people," he writes, "you shall say, thus says the Lord: behold, I set before you the way of life and the way of death.... For I have set my face against this city for evil and not for good, says the Lord. It shall be given in the hand of the king of Babylon and he shall burn it with fire.... Therefore, thus says the Lord: execute you justice and righteousness and deliver the spoiled out of the hand of the oppressor and do no wrong, do no violence to the stranger, the fatherless, nor the widow, nor shed innocent blood in this place..." (Jer. 21:8—22:3).

The Psalms from beginning to end sing of this Way of Life, and show to this day the kind of teaching that took place among the Hebrews. Let us conclude with a few verses of Psalm 119. "Happy are they that are upright in the way, who walk in the law of the Lord..., that seek him with their whole heart. Yea, they do no unrighteousness. They walk in his ways...wherewithal shall a young man keep his way pure? By taking heed thereto according to your word. With my whole heart have I sought you; O let me know...from your commandments. Your word have I laid up in my heart, that I might not sin against you. Blessed are you, O Lord; teach me your statutes...I will meditate on your precepts, and have respect unto your ways" (Psalm 119).

From these samplings of the Law and the Prophets, it is clear that the Hebrews raised their children by a specific kind of teaching that formed them and shaped them and guided them unto a free choice of this Way of Life, consciously and deliberately chosen because of its goodness, chosen out of fidelity to Yahweh, becoming persons by holding themselves on this higher level, free of that other way, the contrasting Way of Death.

This Way of Life rests upon insight and understanding communicated by the revealed Word of God. This insight and understanding turns about certain fundamental truths. The first truth is the reality of the supreme transcendent Creator. The second truth is insight into the nature of man, the creature and child of God, who has been created with this fundamental power of choice between the Two Ways. It is a view upon reality and upon human life, therefore, which sees human actions as appropriate to this humanity which almighty God has called into existence and into the exercise of freedom in choosing the way of life. For life is constituted by human actions, and the quality of human life results from these actions. The Way of Life, therefore, is a way constituted by human actions that conform to the Law of God. The Way of Death is a way of actions which disregard God and hence fall away from Him. It is difficult to overemphasize the importance of this recognition that human actions receive a moral quality from their relationship to Him who is man's Creator. It is the Creator Himself who places man in the moral universe which results from the conscious choice of the Way of Life, in contrast to a choice of the Way of Death.

It remains to ask whether this doctrine of the Two Ways, the practical basis of a teaching that forms children unto the God of Revelation, was continued in Christianity. The answer is perfectly clear.

"Do not think," Jesus Christ says categorically in the Sermon on the Mount, "that I have come to destroy the Law or the prophets. I have not come to destroy, but to fulfill" (Mt. 5:17). He made the commandments of the moral law His own in a personal way, saying: "If you love me, keep my commandments" (Jn. 14:15). Again: "Abide in my love. If you keep my commandments you will abide in my love..." (Jn. 15:10).

The teaching of Jesus Christ becomes luminously clear in the basic clash with the Pharisees summarized in Mark, chapter seven. For they had encrusted the revealed Word of God on the moral Way of Life in so many merely human traditions and separatist national customs that their mission to give the Way of Life to all the pagan

Gentile nations was being frustrated. "And when they saw that some of his disciples were eating bread with defiled (that is, unwashed) hands, they found fault" (Mk. 7:2). St. Mark points out that they were speaking out of the tradition of the ancients, for there have been handed down to them many things to observe. Jesus cuts quickly to the heart of the matter: "Well do you nullify the commandment of God, that you may keep your own tradition"(Mk. 7:9). After explaining to the crowd the difference between the externals of merely human custom and the interior defilement which results from disregard for the revealed Word of God, he entered the house with His disciples. They began to ask Him about the matter. "And he said to them, 'Are you also, then, without understanding? Do you not realize that nothing from outside, by entering a man, can defile him? For it does not enter his heart, but his belly, and passes out into the drain.' Thus he declared all foods clean. 'And,' he said, 'the things that come out of a man are what defile a man. For from within, out of the heart of men, come evil thoughts, adulteries, immorality, murders, thefts, covetousness, wickedness, deceit, shamelessness, jealousy, blasphemy, pride, foolishness. All these things come from within, and defile a man' " (Mk. 7:18-23).

At one stroke the Messiah restores the revealed moral law, the Way of Life, and opens it to all the peoples of the earth. The Way of Life is constituted by human moral actions as such, and it is independent of times and places, of cultures and the development of culture. For this way of moral purity and undefilement has been constituted by the Creator, who made man in His nature and dignity and destiny, and who bids him to live in a way of actions that harmonizes with this nature and expresses its dignity and destiny.

From Moses to Jesus, then, the position of the Catholic Church in catechetics begins to stand revealed: for it is one and the same, the teaching of the same Way of Life that the revealed Word of God lays before men, only now it is universalized, communicated to all men by the Church sent to teach all nations. Catechesis in the Catholic Church is the on-going diligent teaching of this Way of Life to children, raising them in an atmosphere of formation impregnated with revealed truth on God the Father Almighty, Creator of each of us human persons, and on man's dignity of free choice in taking up the way that leads to Him, to ultimate blessedness and happiness. The formation of children in this teaching is the heritage of revealed religion as such, ministered now in the fullness of time to all the Gentile nations by the universal Church which issued forth from Judaism when the Messiah came "him of whom Moses in the Law and the prophets wrote" (Jn. 1:45).

The Epistles of St. Paul document the manner in which the Catholic Church preserves the catechetical teaching program based upon the Two Ways. These Epistles are divided characteristically into two parts. The first half is an explanation of Christian doctrine, showing how the Redemption worked by Jesus Christ fulfills all the prophets and carries out the plan of Yahweh for mankind. The second half is always the practical catechetical conclusion, urging his converts to be confirmed in the Way of Life, now a luminous new possibility because of the ever-present reality of the grace of Christ in the Holy Spirit whom He sends. Thus the New Testament functions entirely under the sign of fulfillment. The Way of Life is now constituted in its fullness: it has become an immediate possibility for each man's freedom because of the grace of Christ. Let one passage from St. Paul to the Ephesians suffice to illustrate. "This, therefore, I say and testify in the Lord, that henceforward you are not to walk as the Gentiles walk in the futility of their mind, having their understanding clouded in darkness, estranged from the life of God through the ignorance that is in them, because of the blindness of their heart. For they have given themselves up in despair to sensuality, greedily practicing every kind of uncleanness. But you have not so learned Christ...taught in him...to put off the old man, which is being corrupted through its deceptive lusts. But be renewed in the spirit of your mind, and put on the new man, which has been created according to God in justice and holiness of truth.... Be you, therefore, imitators of God.... Immorality and every uncleanness or covetousness, let it not even be named among you, as becomes saints; or obscenity or foolish talk or scurrility, which are out of place. For know this and understand, that no fornicator, or unclean person, or covetous one (for that is idolatry) has any inheritance in the kingdom of Christ and God. Let no one lead you astray with empty words; for because of these things the wrath of God comes upon the children of disobedience. Do not, then, become partakers with them.... Walk as children of light...and have no fellowship with the unfruitful works of darkness, but rather expose them. For of the things done by them in secret it is shameful even to speak.... See to it therefore, brethren, that you walk with care: not as unwise but as wise...(and) understand what the will of the Lord is" (Eph. 4:17—5:16).[5]

With transforming power the Church of the Apostles, headed by Peter and Paul, took this revealed doctrine of the Two Ways out of Palestine to the surrounding Gentile peoples. It was the practical application of evangelization; and it was the substance of the catechetical teaching which deepened personal conversion in response to the call of the Gospel.[6] There is rich documentation in the earliest Christian writers for the fact that the catechesis of the Early Church used this teaching of the Two Ways as the heart of instruction in the catechumenate. Let us confine ourselves in illustration to one of the earliest documents, the famed, recently-discovered and priceless *Didache*, or *Doctrine of the Twelve Apostles*.[7]

"Two ways there are," the *Didache* begins, "one of life, and one of death, and there is a great difference between the two ways.... Now the way of life is this: first, love the God who made you; secondly, your neighbor as yourself. Do not do to another what you would not wish to be done to yourself" (1, 1-2).[8]

The *Didache* continues its catechetical teaching by explaining "the lesson of these words" (1, 3). Then it gives detailed actions which Christians are to do, measuring up to their calling and to the way of life which they are embracing with the new grace and power of Christianity, and actions which they are to avoid. Let us give a few examples.

"Abstain from gratifying the carnal and bodily impulses" (1, 4).

"A further commandment of the teaching: do not murder, do not commit adultery, do not practice pederasty; do not fornicate; do not steal; ...do not kill a fetus by abortion or commit infanticide...do not bear false witness...do not be covetous or rapacious or hypocritical or malicious or arrogant..." (2, 107).[9]

"Shun evil of any kind...," the *Didache* continues; "do not be prone to anger, for anger leads to murder...do not be lustful, for lust leads to fornication. Do not be foul-mouthed or give free reign to your eyes; for all these things beget adultery. Abhor all sham and whatever is not pleasing to the Lord.... Such is the way of life" (3-4).[10]

Catholic parents and teachers always have known by direct observation and by the good judgments of common sense, that children are two things at once. They are fully and completely human throughout all their stages of growth and maturation. At the same time, they are blessed with a characteristic innocence in matters of human sexuality during the primary and intermediate years of this growth and maturation.

These are the vital years for their formation unto the Way of Life. Tacitly, because they are fully human and at the same time innocent, they recognize and accept the fact of human sexuality, and at the same time they readily recognize a different and higher purpose for human existence than human sexuality. Hence it is easy to catechize children, giving them the doctrine which bears witness to Jesus as God their Lord, as their Creator, Redeemer and Savior. Coming to know Him, they learn to know, to imitate and to follow also His holy Virgin Mother and St. Joseph.

Jesus, Mary and Joseph are the companions of Catholic children when they are properly catechized, and with them all the saints, persons who are models and examples and paradigms in the imitation of Jesus, Mary and Joseph. Jesus, Mary and Joseph are persons who transcend the use and practice and expression of human sexuality, model personalities who make real and actual the truth that we humans are more than our bodies. Since apostolic times the Catholic Church has been assisting parents to take advantage of these blessed primary and intermediate years of human maturation, in order to give the children what they need most, the full heritage of this divinely-revealed religion with its insight and its strength for embracing the Way of Life in the fullest exercise of human freedom.

Since Sigmund Freud and his school, there has been concerted research upon the dimension of human existence called sexuality. Much of this research, due in no small measure to the predispositions of the Freudian School, has been devoted to sexuality among children. To the surprise of many investigators, a consistent pattern emerged in the findings. There is a period in the life of children "when sexual curiosity and strivings are dormant or latent."[11] Hence there is now common use of the medical term, "the latency period." It is fundamentally important both in the normal psycho-sexual development of children, and in the learning process. This is doubly and triply true when the learning process is that of coming to know the doctrine of the Catholic Faith and the persons to whom that doctrine bears the apostolic witness. For it is this doctrine of the Savior and His cross, together with the grace of the Holy Spirit whom He sends in prayer and the sacraments of His Church, that gives the child the power of human freedom in continuing his personal decision for the Way of Life, in the stormy test that is certain to come when the latency period of human development is over "The child in his latency," writes Dr. Melvin Anchell, M.D., "is educationally ideal."[12]

While learned investigators may sometimes have been surprised at the nature of the evidence for the latency period in human maturation, parents were not surprised. Common sense observation has known this throughout all the centuries of human time. It simply means that children are innocent. And teachers faithful to the heritage of the Judaeo-Christian revelation were likewise not surprised. It is the Creator Himself who makes children to be in this way, giving them this blessed period for acquiring their Christian character, for formation unto the Way of Life, for coming to know, with Jesus, Mary and Joseph, that we humans are more than our bodies and that sexuality, while a fact of life, is not the purpose of life.

The Catholic Church, then, does indeed have a position in catechetics. It is the doctrine of the Two Ways. And this position does indeed touch human sexuality, but not in the manner which shallow mentalities frequently suppose today. It touches it in connection with the innocence of children, now rediscovered by medical science and given a technical label as "the latency period." And it proposes to parents and to teachers this fundamental truth, as old as Adam and Eve, as new as the Church of tomorrow: do not, for the love of God and the children, ever let anyone cause you to fail to take care of the children during their latency period, pastoral and catechetical care, as their Creator intends.

II
The Way of Death

From the call of Abraham, therefore, to the present moment of the ordinary and universal Magisterium of the Church of God, these two contrasting ways have been standing against each other, the Way of Life, and the

Way of Death.[13] These ways are constituted by ways of human living, and human life is made up of human acts, consciously and deliberately willed.

Is the Way of Death identified in the documents of divine Revelation? Are the actions, the qualitative kinds of human acts which constitute it, made clear for all to see? To ask the question is to answer it. One might say that the entire Bible is an identification of morally evil acts, together with the call to human freedom to turn away from them resolutely, by the very act of turning to Yahweh, the God of divine Revelation, the God of human wholeness and virtue, the God of holiness. What else is the *metanoia* for which Jesus calls in the first word of His public life? (Mk. 1:14-15)

Strangely enough, strange at least in an atmosphere that no longer believes in the proneness of fallen human nature toward moral evil, the Chosen People of the Old Law were constantly falling back into the paganism of the surrounding culture. Disregarding the covenant with Yahweh and the religious teaching of their prophets, they kept returning to sing the Rose Song of the Egyptians: "By chance we have come into existence, and afterwards we shall be as if we had not been; for the breath of our nostrils is smoke, and thought is a spark begotten by the heat of our heart; when it is extinguished, the body will disintegrate into ashes and the spirit will vanish into thin air" (Wis. 2:2-3).

We today would call this way of thinking existentialist phenomenology and set it forth in a different verbal dress. But the fundamental thinking is the same. When the original faith in God is lost, faith in God the Father Almighty, Creator of heaven and earth, the immediate consequence is loss of the truth on man's nature, spirituality, immortality and destiny. Matter is all there is, and it is eternally simply there. If there are gods, they did not create it, but can only shape it this way and that. So too each man. In practice he becomes a law unto himself, indeed unto his fallen self. Each man shapes the stuff, the matter of his own life, as if he were himself God and the arbiter of the moral order. He lives as if there were no God, no judgment, no hereafter. He evaluates his actions simply as experiencings in time, and finds them good or bad according to the way they minister to what he considers, according to the cultural ideology and terminology fashionable at his place and time, a full and mature temporal existence. The key to his mentality is the fact that this evaluation prescinds from Creation and proceeds as if there were no God. At most it will concede only that if there is a "god" of some kind, he must surely think in this same sweetly reasonable and truly humanistic way. It is simply incredible to conceive of Him as the universal Creator, placing laws in His Creation, and taking a rightful position as the Judge of human acts.

Prophet after Prophet in Israel rose to recall the people to the Way of Life which their revealed religion taught them, and always it was a struggle. For the Hebrews were a minority, one small people immersed in an ocean of surrounding pagan peoples, often more highly developed in terms of earthly human culture. When the Messiah came, He confirmed their mission, as we have seen, and launched with divine power a movement for the conversion of these same pagans. This is why the *Didache,* this founding document of the position of the Catholic Church in catechetical teaching, contrasts the Way of Death exactly as the Prophets whom Jesus Christ fulfilled. "The way of death is this, wicked and altogether accursed: murders, adulteries, lustful desires, fornications, thefts,...robberies...hypocrisy, duplicity... the lack of the fear of God. It is the way of the persecutors of the good, haters of the truth, lovers of falsehood: in a word, of men steeped in sin.... May you be preserved from all this!"[14] This has been the position of the Catholic Church in her ordinary and universal catechetical teaching and formation of children since the Apostles.

It may come as a surprise, therefore, to learn that the recent book "commissioned by the Catholic Theological Society of America" rationalizes the acceptability of the actions which have been consistently branded as the

Way of Death throughout the entire course of sacred history from Genesis "down to the present period of Church history." [15] This "Study" stands in quite explicit contestation with the living Magisterium, with the documents of the Magisterium throughout the Twentieth Century and in particular with the *Declaration on Sexual Ethics* of December 29, 1975.[16] But there are larger perspectives. This self-styled "Study" is in conflict with the entire immense dimension of divine Revelation as such and stands in opposition to the Creator from the beginning of the universe to the present moment of His on-going creative activity.

For God is one and the same throughout the entire space—time continuum, as mathematical physics now calls this visible cosmos. The souls, furthermore, whom He creates today on the occasion of human parental cooperation with Him, are qualitatively the same human persons, "beings endowed with reason." [17]

God calls to the human mode of existence, that of a spiritual nature incarnate in a body, a mode that enjoys the dignity and responsibility of moral freedom, a freedom that is realized and actualized in the choice between those same two ways, the Way of Life contrasting with the Way of Death. This creative action of God calling this kind of human person into existence, with a way of actions of these two kinds, is the same yesterday, today and will continue the same into the future.[18]

The question must be asked at this point, whether this "Study Commissioned by the Catholic Theological Society of America" enters upon its program of contestation against revealed truth as such, because of new factual knowledge discovered by the empirical sciences which have made so much progress in recent times. The authors themselves enter a disclaimer. "Empirical research to date," they write, "has provided only inconclusive data on the issues concerning this study."[19] The empirical sciences, in other words, are not the source of their position.

Whence then does this contestation come? From theology? It cannot come from a theology which defines itself as a mode of thinking within the magisterium, consciously faithful to divine Revelation contained in Sacred Scripture and divine Tradition. The reason is precisely the contestation of the magisterium, which does no more than propose this revealed Word of God as times and occasions demand.

It remains that the source of this contestation is philosophy. This is definitely the case, as analysis of the publication makes clear. The advocacy of these actions which the Word of God places on the way of death, is a philosophically based advocacy. For these authors embrace and put to use a philosophy which studiously omits God the Father Almighty, the Creator of the human person and hence the Lawgiver of the actions of human persons.

Research in the field of catechetics cannot but take up this matter with vital and professional interest. For the first article of the Apostles' Creed, the foundation of all evangelization and catechesis, is at stake. The fact of the matter is quite clear. From the viewpoint of fundamental metaphysics, there are two kinds or modes of philosophy. One is open to the transcendent reality of an intelligent Supreme Being, and is willing to study the fact that He is the source of all existence as such. This philosophical openness to God the Creator, as a matter of historical record and fact, has been developed most fully and lucidly in the schools and classical works of Christian philosophy.

The other kind or mode in philosophy is characterized by varying degrees of disinclination, disinterest or disregard for God the Creator. It tends to be more concerned with the organization and control of the cosmos, and especially with man's place and role in the cosmos. Beginning with Descartes and Spinoza, ripening in Hume and Kant, generalized in Higher Education throughout the nineteenth century and popularized in the twentieth, this immanentism evaluates human actions from within

the viewpoint of human subjectivity, of existential phenomenology, and studiously avoids, one way or another,
any question of a Word of God.[20] This philosophical
mode of disregard for the Supreme Being, which disdains
His position as the Creator and Lawgiver of human existence, finds two expressions in recent times. The first we
may call the forthright statement, for it expresses explicitly its disdain and denial of the Creator. It has many exponents in the literature of our day. One of the best
known and most influential of these is Jean-Paul Sartre.
Let us see in his work *Existentialism and Humanism* how
he advocates the evaluation of human actions.

"When we think of God as the Creator," Sartre
writes, "we are thinking of Him, most of the time, as a
supernal artisan...so that when God creates He knows
precisely what He is creating. Thus, the conception of
man in the mind of God is comparable to that of the
paper-knife in the mind of the artisan: God makes man
according to a procedure and a conception...Thus each
individual man is a realization of a certain conception
which dwells in the divine understanding."[21] Rejecting
this concept, Sartre continues with a forthright expression
of declared atheism. "Atheistic existentialism," he writes,
"of which I am a representative, declares...that if God
does not exist there is' at least one being whose existence
comes before its essence, a being which exists before it can
be defined by any conception of it. That being is man, or
as Heidegger has it, the human reality. What do we mean
by saying that existence precedes essence? We mean that
man first of all exists, encounters himself, surges up in the
world—and defines himself afterwards. If man as the existentialist sees him is not definable, it is because to begin
with he is nothing. He will not be anything until later,
and then he will be what he makes of himself. Thus,
there is no human nature, because there is no God to have
a conception of it. Man simply is."[22]

Sartre is quite logical in refusing any antecedent
moral law in the evaluation of human acts. "Of all the ac-

tions a man may take in order to create himself as he wills to be, there is not one which is not creative of an image of man such as he believes he ought to be. To choose between this or that is at the same time to affirm the value of that which is chosen."[23] "There can no longer be any good *a priori*, since there is no infinite and perfect consciousness to think it.... We are now upon the plane where there are only men."[24] "You are free, therefore choose—that is to say, invent. No rule of general morality can show you what you ought to do: no signs are vouchsafed in this world."[25] "There is this in common between art and morality," Sartre continues, "that in both we have creation and invention. We cannot decide *a priori* what it is that should be done."[26]

"There is no other universe except the human universe," Sartre concludes, "the universe of human subjectivity.... This is humanism, because we remind man that there is no legislator but himself; that he himself, thus abandoned, must decide for himself.... Existentialism is nothing else but an attempt to draw the full conclusions from a consistently atheistic position."[27]

These words express what we may call the forthright statement of existentialist phenomenology, the evaluation of human actions exclusively from the viewpoint of the phenomena of experience, judging them from their consequences for the human subject in the experience of his felt needs.

There is a second way of embracing this same fundamental philosophy, and of putting it to work in human affairs. This other way, less admirable one may be permitted to say, is the deceitful way. It proposes this same philosophical position, with this same disregard and even disdain of God the Creator and Lawgiver of human existence. It is deceitful because it proposes this philosophical position as an updated Christianity, reinterpreted for acceptability for what is rather pretentiously called modern man.[28] This second way is exemplified currently by the "Study Commissioned by the Catholic Theological Society of America."

For in its discussion of its "broadened definition of sexuality," it allows for extra-marital sex as "fostering a *creative growth toward integration*...[which] better expresses the basic finality of sexuality."[29]

"Catholic tradition in evaluating moral behavior," this *Study* continues, "has placed heavy emphasis in recent centuries on the objective moral nature of the given act itself. Particularly with regard to sexuality, it was believed that there is a meaning intrinsic to the very nature of the act itself—a meaning that is absolutely unchangeable and in no way modifiable by extenuating circumstances or special context. Thus, masturbation, any premarital sexual pleasure, adultery, fornication, homosexuality, sodomy, and bestiality were considered intrinsically evil acts, seriously immoral, and under no circumstances justifiable."[30]

This "Study Commissioned by the Catholic Theological Society of America" is a calculated and sustained effort to show that "American Catholic Thought" is taking up "New Directions" which recognize that this was an older mental pattern, now outdated and in fact no longer true. Current studies and empirical data, it says, giving an example, show that "acts of masturbation are found to be helpful, indifferent or harmful to the growth and development of the person as a result of circumstances apart from the act itself."[31]

This philosophical procedure, that of existential phenomenology, is applied throughout the book to all the categories of sexual behavior just mentioned, and all are found to have "special contexts" in which they foster that often-named but never defined principle of "creative growth toward integration," and are therefore acceptable and morally good.[32] This of course sets aside the doctrine of the Two Ways.

The key chapter of the book is entitled "Toward a Theology of Human Sexuality."[33] It is actually not theology at all, but rather an exercise in philosophy of religion—philosophy of religion of an easily-recognizable type. There is perfunctory nod toward God the Creator here and there, indeed, but the chapter, like the book as a whole, is a studied disregard for the idea of creation and hence of "the Christian concept of life,...the sense of responsibility in each human act toward the Supreme Judge who is everywhere, knows everything and sees everything."[34] In one of its rare references to God, the *Study* speaks of "that God-given freedom of response essential to human dignity" which is denied in the approach "from the viewpoint of conformity to predetermined rules or standards."[35] The harmony with Sartre's approach is clear. The fact that the philosophical mentality underlying this *Study* is existentialist phenomenology becomes explicit in the presentation of sexuality as "our fleshly being-in-the-world," the mode whereby an isolated subjectivity reaches out to communion with another subject.[36]

From what point of view, then, are the human actions considered? The answer is clear on page after page of this "Study Commissioned by the Catholic Theological Society of America." The viewpoint taken is that of the human subject who experiences these actions in time. The actions are considered and evaluated from a time-conditioned, time-restricted, time-imprisoned point of view. Thus they will sometimes be attractive, sometimes not, sometimes desirable, sometimes not, sometimes self-liberating, sometimes not, sometimes joyous, sometimes not, and so on. The evaluative criterion for these actions which the Word of God places on the Way of Death, is consistently that of the human being experiencing these actions in time, as if this organismic experiencing in time, exactly Heidegger's *Dasein*, Being-in-the-World, were all there is to the human mode of existing.

It is fundamental in judging the philosophical orientation of this *Study* to recognize that it nowhere acknowledges the Creator in His Lordship over what He creates, nor asks what the qualitative nature of His creation is, of that creature in particular which we call the human person. Hence the qualitative reference of the actions of the human person to Almighty God is simply omitted.[37]

Catechetics is a field of study constituted in its material and formal aspects by the Articles of Faith: What they are in themselves, and how they are handed on effectively to others by teaching.[38] There are two aspects of this "Study Commissioned by the Catholic Theological Society of America" which challenge catechetical research and practice in a special way, and which one can be sure will increasingly engage younger scholars in this field.

The first aspect is its deceptiveness. It is deceptive on several counts, each of which challenges careful research and clear exposition, without which the current chaos and confusion in religious education can only deepen.

The *Study* begins with an abusive treatment of Sacred Scripture, which it presents as a mere set of "culturally conditioned instructions [which] cannot claim validity for all time."[39] Since the divine plan of revelation and redemption is historical and indeed incarnational in mode, the Word of God is of course inserted concretely into history, communicated in human words of particular places and times. But as the Word of God it has an abiding meaning which transcends the human mode and circumstances of cultural dress and linguistic expression. It is deceptive to promote a confusion of this kind, which operates in practice to set aside the catechetical doctrine of the Two Ways.[40]

It is an abusive treatment of the development of doctrine, furthermore, to portray the history of human thought as a gradual movement toward the doctrine proposed by this "Study Commissioned by the Catholic Theological Society of America." This is not the Catholic concept of the homogeneous evolution of Catholic dogma, nor is it what John Henry Newman discussed in his *Essay on the Development of Doctrine*. The chapter in this *Study* on "Christian Tradition and Human Sexuality" is deceptive.[41] It calls for research and exposition that is clear and explicit, speech in the mode of *Yea, yea, Nay, nay* regarding the Articles of Faith and the development of doctrine.

The same deceptiveness, with even greater pressure upon contemporary persons, characterizes the slanted use made of the empirical sciences.[42] The deception lies in the question put to these sciences: "Is there any behavior that of itself defeats the growth of a creative and integrated personality?"[43] When they are declared to provide "only inconclusive data,"[44] the unwary reader is led to conclude that the teaching of the Church on the natural law is no longer tenable. The empirical sciences are subtly interpreted as speaking for the philosophical approach of existentialist phenomenology. This is highly deceptive, with a deception that only rigorous analysis by philosophical wisdom open to the Supreme Being can unmask.[45]

The use made of Vatican II in general is deceptive, and in particular the distortion of *Gaudium et spes*, no. 51, so as to make it appear to mean the "principle of creative integration." This has been called rightly a betrayal of the teaching of the Council. This is a particular kind of deception, indeed, and it calls for careful and objective research.[46]

Jesus Christ is mentioned somewhat more frequently in the *Study* than God the Creator, but His presence is both rare and unreal. For He is cast in the light of "really" supporting the doctrine of this "Study Commissioned by the Catholic Theological Society of America" and its "principle of creative integration."[47] This way of using Jesus Christ is not only deceptive, but has something blasphemous about it. The matter calls for updated research programs that come to grips with the real issues facing the Catholic Church as this twentieth century verges towards its close.[48]

Jesus Christ is divine charity present with us. His kindness and forgiving spirit always have animated priestly work in the pastoral care of souls. This *Study* has a concerned tone that seems to breathe this spirit, and indèed to be Vatican II as it were in action. "Its efforts," Father Casey writes, "seem to spring not only from a genuine love of Christ and mankind but also from a beautiful compassion for all men and a healthy, positive outlook on life and sexuality."[49] Without any idea of judging subjective sincerity, one must ask whether objectively there can be pastoral care of souls apart from the catechesis of the Two Ways. If not, then this very tone of the *Study* becomes part of the deception.

It has been remarked that God the Creator is hardly mentioned in this *Study*, and in the rare nods to Him, it is as if He quite ingeniously had in mind the "New Directions in American Catholic Thought" which are being proposed. This too is deceptive, by the deception which makes use of existentialist phenomenology in moving synthetically "Toward a Theology of Human Sexuality."[50] It is deceptive to use an alien philosophy in the *doctrina sacra* of the Catholic Church, thus producing a mental construct which has the surface appearance of "theology" but which is actually an exercise in philosophy of religion. This is intellectual deception of the first order, and calls for careful work by a new and intellectually-liberated generation of Catholic scholars. For there is literally no intellectual excuse in this twentieth century for this effort to introduce existentialist phenomenology into the *doctrina sacra* of the Catholic Church. The metaphysics of Heidegger and Sartre belongs to the nineteenth century, and is cut from philosophical cloth as old as Spinoza and Proclus and Plotinus. This old-fashioned belief in the eternity of matter, this studied philosophical disregard for God the Creator, is not a viable position in the twentieth century. The philosophy in this "Study," like that of its secular prototypes, proceeds as if the scientific breakthroughs of the present century had never taken place. These philosophical mentalities seem never to have heard that the contingency of this entire universe has been discovered in our time as a scientific fact, and that the time has been calculated before which this visible cosmos did not exist. Updated thinking must necessarily have a new openness toward God the Creator of existence as such, and toward the renewal of the Christian philosophy which always has cultivated, on purely metaphysical grounds, this recognition regarding existence as such.[51]

There is a second aspect of this "Study Commissioned by the Catholic Theological Society of America" which challenges catechetical research on the part of this new generation of Catholic scholars who are bound to come in the years and decades ahead. This is the element of surprise for the laity that such a doctrine could be presented within the Church as if it were authentic Catholic Christianity for modern man. It is a surprise that shocks and even alienates the laity, as various indicators of thought and practice already have begun to reveal, not excluding the cockle of separatist movements which is being sown upon the field already seeded by the centuries-long apostolate of the Ordinary and Universal Magisterium of the Catholic Church. This is a call for research, therefore, which has a practical urgency, for only thus can this element of shock and surprise, especially where children are concerned, be turned into understanding and renewed dedication to Christocentrism and the Two Ways in catechesis.

For it must necessarily come as a surprise to the Catholic laity, busy with their various callings in society, that this philosophical position and its deceptions should be proposed by persons of the Catholic cloth.[52] It does not come as a surprise, however, to persons of the cloth who follow in ecclesiastical studies the internal affairs of the Catholic Church. The fact is well known that the Catholic Church in the First Vatican Council a century ago undertook out of pastoral concern to come to grips with this atheistic philosophy resurgent in Western Higher Education which rationalizes the Way of Death. It was a doctrinal problem created by a group of priests in Germany, professors on the university level, which as a matter of fact became the immediate occasion for the calling of Vatican I by the Holy See. For these priests had adopted Modern Philosophy, with its Principle of Immanence, instead of Christian Philosophy as the foundation of their approach in Sacred Doctrine. In order to implement the constitutions of Vatican I, Pope Leo XIII for explicit pastoral reasons launched a program of renewal of Christian Philosophy in all the colleges, universities and seminaries of the Catholic Church.[53] Students of Catholic higher education from the inside know well that this call of the Holy See for fundamental renewal in basic philosophical thinking was not obeyed universally within the Church. There was a tacit and hidden disobedience from the beginning. This disobedience affected formation in practically every religious order in the Church, and was visible among professors in the seminaries of the diocesan clergy. This hidden fact of tacit disobedience to the call of the Holy See in this area of fundamental thinking regarding the Supreme Being came to the surface and public visibility in 1933 at the Juvisy Conference on Christian Philosophy in Paris.[54] Since that date there has been a growing internal crisis in the Church's teaching programs, especially in those which are combined with the formation of her own priests and religious.

The "Study Commissioned by the Catholic Theological Society of America" is no surprise in this context; in fact, it becomes readily intelligible. It is simply another milestone in the record of this unfortunate intellectual disobedience to the God of Revelation, the God who speaks and admonishes by the teaching voice of His Church: disobedience on the part of many sons and daughters of this same Church, now grown inveterate, widespread and deepseated as the decades of the twentieth century have proceeded. Always it is the stubborn desire to introduce existentialist phenomenology (and now Marxist Hegelianism as well) as preferable to Christian Philosophy for use in *sacra doctrina*. This puts the person of the cloth into conflict with the mind of the Church. Everything in this *Study*, and all the comments made in the lectures of this series, follow with rigorous logical consequence. The Catholic laity, assisted by all persons of the cloth who intend not to bend the knee to Baal, need to study this phenomenon in depth, in order to eliminate the demoralizing factor of shock and surprise.

Does this phenomenon in general and the *Study* in particular have any specific and serious significance for catechetical teaching? It does indeed. For it quite obviously subverts the catechesis of the Two Ways, relegating the once-cherished Way of Life to an intellectually and culturally outmoded past, and after a paradigm whispered originally in the Garden of Eden, declaring the Way of Death not only quite harmless, but also the positive and mature Way of Creative Growth and Integration. This cannot but affect adult catechetics. But it also affects the catechesis of Catholic children in so special a way that it must be called the new religious education threat to the Catholic child as such. It becomes a threat in the following way, by the unhappy convergence of two factors.

The first factor is the cessation of doctrinal teaching in catechetics proper under the influence of modish new approaches which are actually only an extended naturalistic pre-catechesis, forever extending the positive content of the Catholic Faith into the children's future, and thus omitting it. The Ordinary and Universal Magisterium of the Church stumbles. A silence envelopes the children. They no longer know their religion. The Persons of Jesus, Mary and Joseph are no longer held up to them by sustained, patient and dedicated teaching of the doctrine which is the witness of the Catholic Church to these same Persons, Jesus, Mary and Joseph. The catechetical formation of children which ought to fill the latency period becomes a void.

Then comes the unhappy convergence of the second factor. Into the void thus created, secularized guidance programs shoulder their way to replace sound catechetical teaching. Not surprisingly, the innermost substance of these guidance programs turns out to be precisely this Way of Death, putting them in their formative years on the way advocated by this *Study*.[55] "What is new today," the authors write, "is the systematic programming of sex education, based on the findings of studies in the human sciences and presented through group instruction outside the family."[56]

The convergence of these two factors constitutes a threat to Catholic children of an entirely new dimension and kind. For the intrusion of sexuality of this type and in this way upon the latency period is some kind of violation of nature, and hence of the intention of nature's Author. It is little wonder, then, that parental instincts are aroused, and not only among Catholic parents, to defend the children. For it is natural common sense for parents to recognize this particular danger to their children.[57] Living with their children constantly, they know that they are innocent. In most cases, of course, parents have not studied the psychological research on the latency period, but they do know that it exists in children, that it ought to be protected and not intruded upon, and that during this latency period they ought to be learning the heritage of their religion, becoming a person not in the pathway of this publication but by fidelity to the call of God, imitating the One whom He sent, the Lord Jesus, with His Mother and St. Joseph.

In conclusion, then, one must say that the Catholic Church does have a position in catechetics, and that it does indeed touch the field of human sexuality. The "Study Commissioned by the Catholic Theological Society of America," furthermore, violates this position grievously for all Catholics, not to say all men, and it violates it dangerously for the children. For in their latency years they should be free to be their happy selves, free to acquire their loyalties to Jesus, Mary and Joseph, who personify to them the great truth and reality of creation, that human sexuality is a fact of human existence, but not the purpose of it.

It was the Lord Jesus Himself, who came not to destroy the prophets but to fulfill them, who gave the briefest and most profound answer to the entire problematic under consideration.

"Some Sadducees," St. Mark tells us, "who deny that there is a resurrection,...put [their] question to him.... Jesus said to them, 'Is not the reason why you go wrong, that you understand neither the Scriptures nor the power of God? For when they rise from the dead, men and women do not marry; no, they are like the angels in heaven.... You are very much mistaken' " (Mk. 12:18-27).

Footnotes

1. Cf. Kosnik, Anthony (and others), *Human Sexuality: New Directions in American Catholic Thought.* (New York: Paulist Press, 1977). The title page carries the statement: "A Study Commissioned by the Catholic Theological Society of America."

2. Cf. Sacred Congregation for the Clergy, *General Catechetical Directory* (Washington: United States Catholic Conference, 1971). Part Two, "The Ministry of the Word," nos. 10-35. This phrase recurs throughout the *Directory* as its most fundamental concept. The Word to which catechesis ministers, of course, is the revealed Word of God, of which Jesus Christ is "the Mediator and Fullness." No. 12, citing Vatican II, *Dei Verbum*, no. 2.

3. Jean Daniélou, *Advent* (New York: Sheed and Ward, 1951), p. 35.

4. The Old Testament will be cited in the official Jewish translation of the Masoretic text.

5. Cf. 1 Thes. 1:9: "You broke with idolatry when you were converted to God and became servants of the real, living God." Cf. Karl Hermann Schelkle, *Theology of the New Testament* (Collegeville, Minnesota: The Liturgical Press, 1971), vol. I, pp. 73-74: "The important thing is this, that a man profit by his time, so as not to neglect the hour of God's coming.... History and historicity are, in the Bible, the scope and manner of God's dealings. Therefore does history become, in the biblical concept, the decisive reality. Man must decide his sentence during the hours that are his own. In these historical hours he suffers the gain or the loss of his life." This is a dimension that is characteristically absent from the "Study Commissioned by the Catholic Theological Society of America."

6. Cf. the *General Catechetical Directory, op. cit.*, no. 18: "Catechesis proper presupposes a global adherence to Christ's Gospel as presented by the Church"; and no. 22: "Catechesis performs the function of disposing men to receive the action of the Holy Spirit and to deepen their conversion. It does this through the word, to which are joined the witness of life, and prayer."

7. Cf. James A. Kleist, S.J. (transl.) in *Ancient Christian Writers*, vol. VI (Westminster, Maryland: The Newman Press, 1948); *The Didache*, pp. 1-25. For a detailed discussion and the references, cf. Guy Bourgeault, S.J. *Décalogue et morale chrétienne* (Paris: Desclée, 1971). Pointing out that Leviticus cc. 17-18, with Ex. 20:5-6 and Dt. 5:1-33 establish the priestly mode of teaching in Israel according to the teaching device of the Two Ways, with the Way of Life constituted by respect for the divine commands regarding human actions, and the Way of Death by willful and disobedient disregard for them, Bourgeault concludes, "The *Didache* bears the mark of that ancient theological

insight of Israel" (p. 41). The *Didache* is a fundamental document in establishing the character of catechetical teaching in the Catholic Church, because it underlies the teaching program of the early Church catechumenate. Its basic approach was passed forward and used in all the catechetical treatises and Church Orders which have survived from the Age of the Fathers; and it received its fullest and most comprehensive exposition in St. Augustine's *De catechizandis rudibus;* cf. esp. 21 (37)—25 (48). Cf. E.J. Goodspeed, "The *Didache*, Barnabas and the *Doctrina,*" *Anglican Theological Review* (1945), 228-247; "A basic two-ways teaching program underlies them all, *Didache*, Barnabas, the Church Ordinances, the Nicene faith, and through the *Didache* itself, also the *Didascalia* and the Apostolic Constitutions," p. 228.

8. The New Law expressed in these words clearly continues the heritage of Moses and the prophets, and does not destroy or supplant it; the *shema*, Dt. 6:5 and Lev. 19:18 are tacitly cited.

9. Kleist, *op. cit.,* p. 16.

10. *Ibid.,* pp. 16-18.

11. Sean O'Reilly, M.D. In the *Image of God: A Guide to Sex Education for Parents* (Middleburg, Virginia: Notre Dame Institute Press, 1974), p. 1; "Briefly and simply...this latency period is psychiatric terminology for a phenomenon that is a matter of common sense observation by parents..." *(Ibid.).* "This period or stage, while not a measure of time or age, does coincide more or less with middle childhood, the pre-pubertal years. In the words of the Group for the Advancement of Psychiatry, it is 'a period of apparent quiescence or control of sexual drives occurring between early childhood and adolescence, in which individual development and learning make great strides, and the traditional group culture comes to bear through child-training and educational practices....' (Here) the importance and significance of the latency period are stated" *(Ibid.,* p. 23).

12. Melvin Anchell, M.D. *A Second Look at Sex Education* (Santa Monica: Educulture, 1972); in O'Reilly, *op. cit.,* p. 24.

13. This centuries-long heritage of revealed truth on the divine call of human persons to moral life, the call to choose between the Two Ways, belongs to the very substance of catechesis, and was included in an action of the Extraordinary Magisterium at the First Vatican Council in the Constitution *Dei Filius*, chapter 3: "Since man depends entirely on God as his Creator and Lord, and since created reason is completely subject to uncreated Truth, we are obliged to render by faith full submission of intellect and will to God when He reveals something.... Moreover, all those matters must be believed with divine and Catholic faith that are contained in the Word of God, whether in Scripture or tradition, and that are proposed by the Church, either by a solemn decision or by the Ordinary and Universal Magisterium, to be believed as divinely revealed." Cf. John F. Broderick, S.J., (transl.) *Documents of Vatican Council I* (Collegeville: The Liturgical Press, 1971), pp. 43, 44; for the original text, cf. Denzinger-Schönmetzer 3011.

14. Kleist, *op. cit.,* p. 18.

15. This is the phrase of St. Augustine, stating the basic principle of catechetical methodology in his *De catechizandis rudibus* 3(5); cf. J.P. Christopher (trans.) *The First Catechetical Instruction* (Westminster, Maryland: The Newman Press, 1946), p. 18. The "Study Commissioned by the Catholic Theological Society of America" places itself in conflict with the entire heritage of religious education that has resulted from the existence of a revealed Word of God. For a sampling, cf. Kosnik, *op. cit.,* p. 7 ("The Bible should not be seen as

giving absolute prescriptions with regard to sex"); 154-158 (pre-marital sex can be a morally good experience if it is "loving, responsible"); 178 (sex among voluntary singles: "relationships which foster growth and integration are morally good"); 229-30 (sex with animals is pathological "when hetero-sexual outlets are available"); 214 ("Homosexuals enjoy the same rights... (to) a moral judgment upon his or her relationships and actions in terms of whether or not they are self-liberating, other-enriching, honest, faithful, life-serving and joyous." For the special way "life-serving" is understood, cf. pp. 94-95); and *passim*.

16. Here one thinks also of the *Divini illius Magistri* of Pope Pius XI (1929), *Gaudium et spes*, no. 51 of Vatican II, the *Humanae vitae* of Pope Paul VI (1968), and the several documents of Pope Pius XII on situation ethics.

17. Sacred Congregation for the Doctrine of the Faith, *Declaration on Certain Questions Concerning Sexual Ethics* (Washington: U.S.C.C., 1976), p. 5. Rejecting "the view that so-called norms of the natural law or precepts of Sacred Scripture are to be regarded only as given expressions of a form of particular culture at a certain moment of history," the Holy See in this document teaches that "those many people are in error who today assert that one can find neither in human nature nor in the revealed law any absolute and immutable norm to serve for particular actions other than the one which expresses itself in the general law of charity and respect for human dignity" *(Ibid.)*. The principle by which human actions are to be considered and evaluated is stated with utmost explicitness: "Divine Revelation and, in its own proper order, philosophical wisdom, emphasize the authentic exigencies of human nature. They thereby necessarily manifest the existence of immutable laws inscribed in the constitutive elements of human nature and which are revealed to be identical in all beings endowed with reason." This reasserts today the validity of catechetical teaching upon the historic framework of the Two Ways, and provides for the on-going catechetical importance of the latency period in children as reflecting the mind and intention of the Creator.

18. Cf. *ibid.*, *passim*, and especially no. 13: "It is up to the bishops to instruct the faithful.... It will especially be necessary to bring the faithful to understand that the Church holds these principles not as old and inviolable superstitions, nor out of some Manichaean prejudice, as is often alleged, but rather because she knows with certainty that they are in complete harmony with the divine order of creation and with the spirit of Christ, and therefore also with human dignity."

19. Kosnik, *op. cit.*, p. 77. This is the "conclusion" of Chapter III, "The Empirical Sciences and Human Sexuality," pp. 53-77. "Culture," the authors explain, "obviously plays a significant role in determining what, to our visceral judgment, shall appear 'natural' or 'deviant' " *(Ibid.)*. It would be difficult to state more clearly the philosophical intention to disregard any purported "Word of God" addressing the actions and expressions of human sexuality: the criterion of truth has become "our visceral judgment." This sets the stage objectively for a turn to Jean-Paul Sartre for help in perceiving the nature of the philosophy which provides the hidden metaphysical substrate of this "Study."

20. For the comprehensive study of this phenomenon, cf. Cornelio Fabro, *God in Exile: A Study of the Internal Dynamic of Modern Atheism from Its Roots in the Cartesian Cogito to the Present Day* (New York: Newman Press, 1968); esp. pp. 1061-1085, "The Virtual Atheism of the Principle of Immanentism." And Georg Siegmund, *God on Trial: A Brief History of Atheism* (New York: Desclee, 1967); esp. pp. 13-77, "The Struggle between Belief and Unbelief," and pp. 119-168, "The Metaphysical Revolt."

21. Jean-Paul Sartre, *Existentialism and Humanism* (London: Methuen, 1957), p. 27.

22. *Ibid.*, pp. 27-28.

23. *Ibid.*, p. 29.

24. *Ibid.*, p. 33.

25. *Ibid.*, p. 38. Vatican II, in its document *Presbyterorum Ordinis* (Dec. 7, 1965), on the Ministry and Life of Priests, no. 18, has an almost *verbatim* rejection of the Sartrian doctrine; cf. Austin Flannery (ed.), *Vatican Council II: The Conciliar and Post-Conciliar Documents* (Collegeville, Minnesota: The Liturgical Press, 1975), pp. 896-897.

26. *Ibid.*, p. 49.

27. *Ibid.*, pp. 55-56. It is significant that Sartre attaches this doctrine to Modern Philosophy as such, in a passage, p. 44, that could have been written by Cornelio Fabro: "Our point of departure is, indeed, the subjectivity of the individual.... At the point of departure (in philosophy) there cannot be any other truth than this, *I think, therefore I am*, which is the absolute truth of consciousness as it attains to itself. Every theory which begins with man, outside of this moment of self-attainment, is a theory which thereby suppresses the truth, for outside the Cartesian *cogito*, all objects are no more than probable.... Before there can be any truth whatever, then, there must be an absolute truth, and there is such a truth which is simple, easily attained and within the reach of everybody; it consists in one's immediate sense of one's self." It is clear that the Supreme Being transcendent over all human selves has not only been denied; He has been replaced by the human Self experiencing existence in time, Heidegger's *Dasein*. This human Self knows good and evil in its experiencing because it places there its own law for its own "creative growth toward integration," the principle that recurs throughout the "Study Commissioned by the Catholic Theological Society of America," and which is stated formally on pp. 86-87.

28. St. Boniface considered himself a "modern man" in the eighth century when he was converting the Germans in the forests near Fulda, using the term *nos moderni* in his letters to the Successor of St. Peter in Rome. One can wonder whether this current use of the term will be valid fifty years hence, or five hundred? Suppose younger scholars arise who find that the approach of the "Study" commissioned by the Catholic Theological Society of America is not viable in terms of true and integral humanism? Suppose they subject it to analysis and find it philosophically dated, culturally parochial? For what is to prevent younger scholars from discovering, with the help perhaps of astrophysics, a different kind of philosophical wisdom, more open to the Creator, and better able to recognize quite different exigencies of human nature?

29. Kosnik, *op. cit.*, p. 86; his emphasis.

30. Kosnik, *ibid.*, p. 88.

31. Kosnik, *ibid.*

32. Cf. the sampling in note 15, above. Many others could be added. For a particularly revealing passage, see p. 179, the discussion of "swinging singles."

33. Kosnik, *op. cit.*, Chapter IV, "Toward a Theology of Human Sexuality," pp. 78-98.

34. Pope St. Pius X, in his *Catechism of Christian Doctrine* (Middleburg, Virginia: Notre Dame Institute Press, 1975), p. 115. God is mentioned at two other points in the chapter, once on p. 86, where sexuality is said to humanize people and so to be "commensurate with their vocation to be and to become the image of God"; and on p. 85, where God is congratulated: "Sexuality is the Creator's ingenious way of calling people constantly out of themselves into relationship with others."

35. Kosnik, *op. cit.*, p. 98.

36. Kosnik, *op. cit.*, p. 83. Cf. pp. 83-88 on "Personhood" and 99-100 on "Sexuality and Personhood" for a treatment in the standard terminology and concepts of Modern Philosophy as such, especially its Vitalist-Existentialist mode elaborated by nineteenth-century Kantians and popularized in recent decades by Heidegger and Sartre. The studied refusal of the ontological, the persistent evaluation of human acts simply as phenomena of the human subject, having meaning simply for the subject's consequent being-in-time, is analyzed accurately by J.H. Casey, S.J., *"Human Sexuality: Dead End of the New Morality," Homiletic and Pastoral Review* (Dec. 1977), 18-28. The *Study* "betrays" *Gaudium et spes*, no. 51, "by substituting 'creative' for 'procreative' " (p. 24). Vatican II is "ontological, not phenomenological" (p. 25). This *Study* refuses to analyze the nature of being a person, in order to discern what actions are appropriate to such a being. All is made to depend on "consequences of actions for consciousness" (p. 25). But this is the "principle of immanentism" in action. Cf. Cornelio Fabro in note 20 above.

37. The *Study* and its existentialist phenomenology were rejected in advance by Vatican II, *The Church in the Modern World*, no. 51; cf. Austin Flannery, *Vatican Council II* (New York: Costello, 1975), p. 955: "Let all be convinced that human life and its transmission are realities whose meaning is not limited by the horizons of this life only: their true evaluation and full meaning can only be understood in reference to man's eternal destiny."

38. This is the central thrust of the *General Catechetical Directory*, hence the widespread dissent from it on the part of the Neo-Modernist movement in religious education. For a detailed study of both this central thrust and the dissent, cf. Marcel Gillet, S.J., *Notre Catéchèse: Pour que nos enfants deviennent les amis de Dieu* (Paris: Tequi, 1975), a work honored by a special approbation from the Holy See.

39. Kosnik, *op. cit.*, p. 7; cf. Chapter I, "The Bible and Human Sexuality," pp. 7-32, *passim*. The lack of authentic biblical scholarship in this chapter has been documented by Manuel Miguens, O.F.M., S.T.D., S.S.D., in his essay above in the present volume.

40. Hence the *General Catechetical Directory*, no. 5, writes as follows: "The Christian faith...has an urgent duty, therefore, to manifest its true nature, by virtue of which it transcends every advancement of culture, and to show forth its newness in cultures which have been secularized and desacralized."

41. Cf. Kosnik, *op. cit.*, pp. 33-52.

42. Cf. Kosnik, *op. cit.*, pp. 53-77, "The Empirical Sciences and Human Sexuality." While admitting that "empirical research to date has provided only inconclusive data on the issues concerning this study," p. 77, the approach alludes to the empirical sciences throughout the lengthy chapter on "Pastoral Guidelines," as if they were a pervasive solid support for taking the "New Directions" and giving up the catechesis of the Two Ways. This is deceptive in a special way for contemporary man, prone as he is, perhaps excusably so, to accept what is said to be "now scientifically known" as indeed factually given.

43. Kosnik, *op. cit.*, p. 56.

44. *Ibid.*, p. 77.

45. What Catholic thought holds on this point is an intellectual constant from the apostles to the present, and was given succinct statement by the Holy See once again in the *Declaration on Sexual Ethics* (December 29, 1975), no. 4; see note 10, above.

46. For the Latin original of the passage in question, cf. *AAS* (Dec., 1966) 1072-1073; "morales igitur indoles rationis agendi...objectivis criteriis, ex personae eius demque actuum natura desumptis, determiniri debet" (p. 1072). Cf. J.H. Casey in note 36 above.

47. Cf., for example, Kosnik, *op. cit.*, pp. 82-83 and 87-88; also pp. 20-22, 30-31 and 96.

48. The very substance of catechetics is at stake, not only the practical teaching in terms of the Two Ways, but also the Christocentrism which is the heart of catechetical methodology. Cf. the *General Catechetical Directory*, no. 40: "Catechesis must necessarily be Christocentric." But a Jesus Christ in the mode of Heidegger and Sartre? Or the divine Christ of the Catholic Creed who fulfills the teaching of the Two Ways proposed to man by the God who creates man in this freedom?

49. J.H. Casey, *op. cit.*, p. 18.

50. Cf. Kosnik, *op. cit.*, pp. 78-98.

51. Cf. Henri Bon, *La création: vérité scientifique au XXe siècle* (Paris: Nouvelles Éditions Latines, 1954); Pierre Loyer, *Du cosmos à Dieu* (Paris: Nouvelles Éditions Latines, 1971); and especially Claude Tresmontant, *Sciences de l'univers et problèmes métaphysiques* (Paris: Editions du Seuil, 1976). Pondering educational tendencies he was already able to recognize, John Henry Newman saw them result in minds "so shallow as not even to know their own shallowness." Cf. *The Idea of a University* (London: Longman's, Green, 1947), p. 132. Newman has lucid pages, which project the future effect of these tendencies upon persons of the cloth. See, for example, *ibid.*, pp. 370-373, on the presence and absence of "true cultivation of mind." It is well known that the *Aeterni Patris* of Pope Leo XIII has the field of academic education in mind; this is a matter open for much comparative study with Newman's educational principles and ideals.

52. Four of the five members of the committee which produced the "Study Commissioned by the Catholic Theological Society of America" are "persons of the cloth," three priests and one religious sister. The chairperson is a priest of the Archdiocese of Detroit and seminary Professor of Moral Theology.

53. Cf. the Encyclical *Aeterni Patris* (August 4, 1879), "On the Restoration of Christian Philosophy in Schools"; in Etienne Gilson (ed.) *The Church Speaks to the Modern World* (New York: Doubleday Image Book, 1954), pp. 29-54. Gilson in his "Introduction" makes it clear that Leo XIII considered this the most important action of his pontificate. It is designed to take pastoral care of young Catholic students, the hope of the Church, in the face of the widespread "varieties of one and the same error, namely, the refusal to recognize the existence of God, of a supernatural order, and of the duty we have to submit to it" (p. 7). A century later one must say that the program is more timely than ever from a pastoral point of view, but that the organizational *locus* for this renewal has shifted from the academic order (still a valid hope from Leo XIII through Vatican II) to the catechetical order, the order of the Articles of Faith as such, together with their effective communication by teaching—even when the teaching is pressed back largely to the level of the homes.

54. Cf. R.P. Deman, O.P. (ed.), *La philosophie chrétienne* (Juvisy: Éditions du Cerf, 1933), the transcript of the *Journée d'études*, Sept. 11, 1933. Two years earlier the general French Society for Philosophy had taken "The Notion of Christian Philosophy" as its topic. Cf. *Bulletin de la Société Française de Philosophie, Seance de 21 Mars, 1931* (Paris: Librairie Armand Colin, 1931). Étienne Gilson was invited to introduce the discussion. As the day went on,

reported *verbatim* in this *Bulletin*, the Catholic lay philosophers Gilson and Maritain engaged in sustained and successful intellectual swordplay with the atheists Brunschvicq and Brehier, who denied the very notion by claiming that the adjective destroys the authenticity of the noun. At the Juvisy Conference Gilson again was present, surrounded this time by persons of the cloth, including many famous names in the Catholic drama of the last forty years. Certain of these persons took in substance the same intellectual position as the atheists Brunschvicq and Brehier had represented at the earlier secular meeting. Gilson reports on this Juvisy Conference and with urbane charity lets his readers know his surprise and shock in his volume *Christianity and Philosophy* (New York: Sheed and Ward, 1939), pp. 82-102. "It is rather disturbing to us," he writes on p. 101, "that, instead of hearing these fundamental truths taught to us as first certitudes, we have today to fight for them, sometimes even against those from whom it seems we ought to be getting them." These words are one of the first statements of what has eventually become a commonplace, the sense of shocked surprise on the part of the Catholic laity generally. It is difficult not to think once again of Newman, with his deep appreciation of the role of the laity, sometimes a suffering one, in the Church of God. "It is a miserable time," he writes in *The Idea of a University (ibid.*, p. 296), when a man's Catholic profession is no voucher for his orthodoxy, and when a teacher of religion may be within the Church's pale, yet external to her faith."

55. Cf. Kosnik, *op. cit.*, "Programs of Sex Education and Formation," pp. 237-239. The "Study Commissioned by the Catholic Theological Society of America" is already giving new life to "Becoming a Person" advocates and approaches. Some documentation of the fact already is at hand. Cf. Carl L. Middleton, Jr., and Robert P. Craig, *Teaching the Ten Commandments Today* (West Mystic, Connecticut: Twenty-Third Publications, 1977; in their "acknowledgments," p. 6, the authors "thank Rev. Anthony Kosnik for sharing his ideas especially in relation to the sixth commandment. Some of these ideas have been adapted from his forthcoming book, *Human Sexuality: New Direction in Catholic Thought*, published by Paulist Press." For an example of the way certain priests are using the book in adult catechetics, cf. *The Catholic Connection* (February, 1978), pp. 4-5, featuring Rev. Thomas J. Quinlan of the Richmond Diocese and his "series of lectures pertaining to 'Human Sexuality,' a recent publication by (sic) the Catholic Theological Society of America...and how it can enrich us." Quinlan's summary of his lectures, *ibid.*, p. 5, is a knee-jerk type of lyrical praise for the Kosnik *Study*.

56. Kosnik, *op. cit.*, p. 237.

57. For an incisive French evaluation of the matter, cf. Claude Tresmontant, *op. cit.*, pp. 210-211, where bad catechetics is placed in the context of abortion and of social systems that produce and distribute insufficient food. "More serious than physical destruction," he writes on p. 211, "worse than physical death, which is not annihilation, is interior and spiritual destruction. One can massacre children by a bombardment, but one can also slowly depress them, demean them, degrade them, turn them from their finality, and that under the influence of the ambient milieu, of the teaching one gives them, of the vision of the world one proposes to them. Along these lines one can degenerate children." Priests and religious have a new privilege and duty, that of assisting Catholic parents in this new internal mission and apostolate in the Church.

Index of Persons and Subjects

Also available:

The Sacrament of the Eucharist in Our Time

Edited by George A. Kelly
  A compact theology of the Eucharist by the faculty of the Institute for Advanced Studies in Catholic Doctrine at St. John's University.
  Aspects treated include the Eucharist in Catholic Tradition; The Eucharist as a Sacrifice; Old and New Conceptions; Christ in the Eucharist; Presence and Reality; Discerning the Body of the Lord; Who May Receive the Eucharist; The Eucharist in Catechesis—Current Approaches. 108 pages
cloth $3.75; paper $2.25 — RA0155

The Sacrament of Penance in Our Time

Edited by George A. Kelly
  In-depth lectures on the sacrament of Reconciliation covering such topics as:

Socio-historical questions about the penitential discipline of the Catholic Church; Penance and the Second Vatican Council; The New Rite of Penance; Penance as renewal and reconciliation, etc. Contributors to this timely book are Robert I. Bradley, S.J., Bruce A. Williams, O.P., Joseph E. Hogan, C.M., Eugene Kevane, John A. Hardon, S.J. 165 pages cloth $4.00 -- RA0160

The Teaching Church in Our Time

Edited by George A. Kelly

Covers the relationship to the magisterium of Catholic doctrine in the following areas—Scripture, Tradition, modernism, infallibility, catechetics and sexual matters. The contributors are Msgr. Eugene Kevane; Fr. Manuel Miguens, O.F.M.; Fr. Robert Bradley, S.J.; Fr. John Hardon, S.J.; Fr. Joseph Hogan, C.M.; Fr. Bruce A. Williams, O.P.; all faculty members for the Institute for Advanced Studies in Catholic Doctrine at St. John's University, New York City.

250 pages; cloth $6.00; paper $4.50 — RA0190

Declaration on Certain Questions Concerning Sexual Ethics

Sacred Congregation for the Doctrine
   of the Faith
   "...The purpose of this Declaration is to
draw the attention of the faithful in
present-day circumstances to certain errors and modes of behavior which they
must guard against." 27 pages
20¢ — PM0500

The Human Body

   666 pronouncements. "Gathers together the teachings of Popes Leo XIII,
Pius XI and Pius XII concerning the
origin, value, education, use and destiny
of the human body." "Catholic Book Review" 435 pages
cloth $6.50 — EP0570

Human Life Is Sacred

Irish Bishops' Pastoral on
   Abortion
   Euthanasia
   Human Sexuality
   Contraception
(With study guidelines.)
   With warm style, this pastoral letter
deals with one of the main topics of our

time. People have always discussed sex, marriage, human dignity and violence but never as openly and as continuously as now. Faced with this non-stop public debate, the Christian may wonder what his religion has to offer. This pastoral letter gives the answer clearly: Human life *is* sacred. 79 pages
paper $1.50 — MS0300

Matrimony

138 pronouncements from Benedict XIV to John XXIII. A valuable reference work for every library; an historical and doctrinal record of the Church's teachings on marriage for the past 225 years. 508 pages
cloth $5.50; paper $4.50 — EP0730

Morality Today—The Bible in My Life

Daughters of St. Paul
A unique way to study the Ten Commandments!
In simple and clear language, but with a very personal approach, each commandment is explained in all its aspects, negative and positive. We are invited to ponder...adore...and speak to God so that through instruction, reflection and

prayer we may understand and love His holy Law.

All will find this book both informative and inspirational.

cloth $3.00; paper $1.95 — SC0088

Natural Family Planning —the 100% Solution

Herbert F. Smith, S.J.

Also includes "Is the Pill on the Way Out?" by Herbert F. Smith, S.J., Dr. Joseph M. Gambescia, M.D. and Albert Vara.

25¢ — PM1315

Of Human Life

Pope Paul VI

Encyclical "Humanae Vitae." 24 pages

15¢ — EP0840

The Sanctity of Human Life

Rev. John A. Hardon, S.J.

This helpful pamphlet leads us to reflect on the meaning of human life and to see God as the author of all human life. 19 pages

15¢ — PM1735

Sexual Inversion: The Questions—With Catholic Answers

Rev. Herbert F. Smith, S.J., with Joseph A. Di Ienno, M.D. Introduction by V. Michael Vaccaro, M.D.

Informative treatments of such topics as: Homosexuality, morality, and religion; homosexuality and the medical sciences; homosexuality and society; living with one's homosexual orientation.

cloth $2.95; paper $1.95 — RA0165

Symposium on the Magisterium: A Positive Statement

Edited by Msgr. John J. O'Rourke and S. Thomas Greenburg

A positive response to the continuing debate about the Magisterium, its meaning, composition, authority and proper function. Among those taking part in the symposium were Cardinal Krol of Philadelphia, Archbishop Whealon of Hartford, Bishop Maloney, Abbot McCaffrey, and others. 152 pages

cloth $5.95; paper $4.50 — RA0185

Please order from any of the addresses on the following page, specifying *title* and *item number*.

Daughters of St. Paul

IN MASSACHUSETTS
  50 St. Paul's Ave. Jamaica Plain, Boston, Ma. 02130
  172 Tremont Street, Boston, Ma. 02111
IN NEW YORK
  78 Fort Place, Staten Island, N.Y. 10301
  59 East 43rd Street, New York, N.Y. 10017
  625 East 187th Street, Bronx, N.Y. 10458
  525 Main Street, Buffalo, N.Y. 14203
IN NEW JERSEY
  Hudson Mall — Route 440 and
    Communipaw Avenue, Jersey City, N.J. 07304
IN CONNECTICUT
  202 Fairfield Avenue, Bridgeport, Ct. 06604
IN OHIO
  2105 Ontario St. (at Prospect Ave.), Cleveland,
    Oh. 44115
  25 E. Eighth Street, Cincinnati, Oh. 45202
IN PENNSYLVANIA
  1719 Chestnut Street, Philadelphia, Pa. 19103
IN FLORIDA
  2700 Biscayne Blvd., Miami, Fl. 33137
IN LOUISIANA
  4403 Veterans Memorial Blvd., Metairie, La. 70002
  1800 South Acadian Thruway, P.O. Box 2028,
    Baton Rouge, La. 70821
IN MISSOURI
  1001 Pine Street (at North 10th), St. Louis, Mo. 63101
IN ILLINOIS
  172 North Michigan Avenue, Chicago, Ill. 60601
IN TEXAS
  114 Main Plaza, San Antonio, Tx. 78205
IN CALIFORNIA
  1570 Fifth Avenue, San Diego, Ca. 92101
  46 Geary Street, San Francisco, Ca. 94108
IN HAWAII
  1143 Bishop Street, Honolulu, Hi. 96813
IN ALASKA
  750 West 5th Avenue, Anchorage, Ak. 99501
IN CANADA
  3022 Dufferin Street, Toronto 395, Ontario, Canada
IN ENGLAND
  57, Kensington Church Street, London W. 8, England
IN AUSTRALIA
  58 Abbotsford Rd., Homebush, N.S.W., Sydney 2140,
    Australia